C000069826

FROM STRESS TO

SUCCESS

How to build a successful business
that operates without you

JOHN PAUL

R∃THINK PRESS

First published in Great Britain 2017
by Rethink Press (www.rethinkpress.com)

© Copyright John Paul

All rights reserved. No part of this publication may be reproduced, stored in or introduced into a retrieval system, or transmitted, in any form, or by any means (electronic, mechanical, photocopying, recording or otherwise) without the prior written permission of the publisher.

The right of John Paul to be identified as the author of this work has been asserted by him in accordance with the Copyright, Designs and Patents Act 1988.

This book is sold subject to the condition that it shall not, by way of trade or otherwise, be lent, resold, hired out, or otherwise circulated without the publisher's prior consent in any form of binding or cover other than that in which it is published and without a similar condition including this condition being imposed on the subsequent purchaser.

CONTENTS

6. Make It Work – Develop A Leadership-centric

Business **139**

PREFACE

I remember the call like it was yesterday. I'd been playing rugby and my father rang to ask if I could come over for a chat. I didn't think anything of it, assuming he just wanted one of our regular catch-ups. The next day, as my brother, my parents and I were sitting round the table, my dad dropped the bombshell on us.

"I have cancer, lads, and it's not looking good."

My whole world fell apart. I didn't know what to say or do, but I mustered the words, "Mam's beaten it; so can you." My mother had had breast cancer a few years before, but she had recovered from it and I was sure he would, too.

Dad said it wasn't good news: it was terminal. It still didn't sink in. This was my dad – my hero, my idol, the man I looked up to so much – telling me he was going to die. I asked how much time he had left and he said he didn't know; he needed to have more tests.

I thought it couldn't get any worse, but it did. When the hospital took the biopsy to see how far the cancer had progressed, Dad got an infection and went downhill quickly. Only two weeks after he told me he had cancer I received a call from my mam to say, "This is it." I rushed over to find my dad struggling to breathe. An ambulance was on the way.

Dad slipped into a coma and died two days later. He did wake for a few hours and, although he was sedated, I got to say my goodbyes, for which I'm thankful. Devastated doesn't even come close. My dad was the glue that bound the family together.

Later that day I went to the factory to tell the staff in person, and pretty much the whole shop floor was in tears. Big, hard men from mining stock were openly crying about the loss of my father. It makes me proud to know he was so well liked and respected.

After Dad died, things went from bad to worse. The company couldn't operate without him. Although he had a management team, he was integral to the business. He only worked half days by then, as he wanted to spend more time at home with my mother after she had had cancer, but he was still making all the important decisions about the direction and operation of the business.

We had crisis meeting with a potential investor (who happened to be a long-term friend of my dad's), the bank manager and other people who we thought could help. Unfortunately, none of them could come up with a solution and the situation got worse. After several meetings, the bank said they couldn't support us any longer and we had to call in the receivers. All the hard work my father and grandfather had put into building the company over the years, had come to nothing.

When he found out he was ill, Dad told us he wanted to sell the business. He thought he would have enough time to see the sale through and he was prepared to sell the business for less than it was worth to secure our financial future. He wanted to set my brother and i up in business while leaving enough money for my mother to live on. Even in his final days he was doing his best to help others, and I have always tried to emulate this trait.

I was the first person to be made redundant by the receivers. My mother was second and my brother was third. Fair play to them: they were only doing their jobs. Within three months we lost my dad, the business, our jobs, our income, our cars and all the perks of running a family business. It was a devastating time. Little did I know that this experience would give me a passion for systems and shape how my future business would run.

I used to think "It'll never happen to me", but as my family found out, it can happen to anyone at any time. My dad aimed to fully retire and then sell the company and he was only a few years away from achieving that, but then the unthinkable happened and we lost everything. That's why you need to make sure you protect your business as much as you can.

I have learned from my experience, and you can too.

INTRODUCTION

When I told my family I was going to write a book, my seven-year-old son Jack asked me what it was going to be about. Always trying to be the good dad who involved him in things, I explained that it was about systems and processes and how they improve your business and your work-life balance. Jack's face went blank as he continued to play with his dinosaurs. At the time, I was slightly disappointed that he hadn't taken more interest in my detailed explanation. But I now know that the same blank expression I saw on my son's face is typical of most owners of small- to medium-sized enterprises when business talk turns to systems and processes. The mere mention of processes or audits is enough to make anyone's eyes glaze over. Jack was in good company.

Unless we've worked in a large corporation or watched several series of *Suits* or *LA Law*, most of us aren't familiar with that type of language. Even though I'm now more familiar with what is known as corporate language, I believe most of the words have no real meaning in everyday English. After all, have you ever read a management report? Some of them are like a cross between Vulcan and Hobbit languages! Corporate jargon sounds impressive, but outside the corporate world it doesn't mean much.

This book sets out a no-nonsense approach to systemising small- to medium-sized businesses. The definition of systemisation will change depending on who you ask, but my definition is: "organising, managing and operating your business in the most efficient and effective way possible whilst serving the client".

When working with businesses of this size, I've found that almost all of them are facing the problems that come from a lack of systemisation. These include poor customer service, staff problems, poor communication, lack of motivation, lack of accountability and cash-flow issues, among others.

It's no one's fault that they don't know about systemising a business. After all, we don't start a business one day and find it's a perfectly well-oiled machine the next day. Business is a continuously evolving process of improvement. The building blocks of every business are its systems. Growth, sales and expansion all stem from the basics. Get those right and the rest is much easier.

I've learned everything I know about systems and procedures by reading books and articles, and this book shares what I have learned. It won't take your business from losing money to floating on the stock exchange, but I believe it will help you take a major step forward in the evolution of your business. By applying the ideas, theories and practical examples in this book, you will see improvements in your business and in your work-life balance. After putting into practice what I have learned I now see more of my children, I'm healthier and I'm back at the gym. I also have more money to spend on enjoying life because I'm no longer bogged down in tasks that don't bring in income.

I love sharing, and most of my family and friends will say I love talking too. I speak at networking events all over the country about business and property topics, but my favourite topic by far is systemising your business. As a working-class lad from humble beginnings in the north-east collieries, I'm proud to have achieved so much through self-education, hard graft and determination. If someone whose previous job was to get punched in the face (I used to be a cage fighter!) can successfully systemise their business, so can you.

I believe there is a gap in business training. The most important aspects of how to run a successful business seem to have been forgotten about. I have three degrees, but I use only a small amount of what I was taught – the rest has come from reading books, articles in the trade press, and articles available online. According to the Federation of Small Businesses, 50% of businesses fail in the first five years. If you and I had neighbouring businesses, the likelihood is that one of us would go out of business. Given that few businesses make any money in the first five years, the chances are that the one who's still in business won't make much money and the other will go bust and owe money.

This book aims to plug the training gap. It will introduce you to a simple five-part system that will free you from the drudgery of running a business and give you back the time to spend with your family and friends while your business grows without you.

My story

Everyone has a story behind what they do. Mine has had a big impact on my values and beliefs and the way I run my business. It also explains my passion for systems and business basics.

I'm proud to say that I come from a working-class background. I grew up in the former pit village of Trimdon in east Durham. When I speak at networking events I always mention where I'm from, as it's certainly shaped the person who I am today. I had a great upbringing, with loving parents and many happy memories. My father had a couple of small companies. One was a mining-engineering company, which, sadly, he had to shut down when Margaret Thatcher closed the pits. The other was a precision-engineering company, Durham Light Industries, which employed about forty staff and made a decent profit. It gave us a pretty good lifestyle, but my dad had to work hard and late at night. He was often away at conferences, although he sometimes took my mother to keep him company.

Dad came to as many cricket and rugby matches as he could. Although he wasn't there as often as I would have liked him to be, I appreciated it every time he made the effort. I knew that he was working to provide for us all.

Thanks to my father's success, we had nice house in the nice part of town. My younger brother Jamie and I went to a good private school. I remember Dad telling me how proud he was that he could afford to give us what he thought was the best education money could buy. Looking back, I'm proud of what my father achieved and the sacrifices he made for us to be educated to a much higher standard than he was.

You could say that I came from entrepreneurial stock. My great-grandfather started a well-known local bus company, Trimdon Motor Services, and my grandfather had a garage there, too. Having said that, almost all my family worked down the pit at some point or in companies related to mining. My father lasted three years down the mine before moving to the chemical plant ICI in Teesside. He worked in the evenings and at weekends to set up his engineering company, making gates and fences out of metal.

It was a hard slog – engineering wasn't easy. But the company grew and my dad eventually constructed his own purpose-built 50,000-foot factory. This made him so happy, and he visited the construction site all the time, taking my brother and me along with him on Sundays. I was in awe of what he had achieved – building his own factory and employing lots of people – but I knew little about the hard work that went with it.

I left school with below-average grades and went to college: my teacher told me not to go to university, because it would be a step too far. I now have three degrees, I'm in the process of doing my Masters so this goes to show I've proved the critics wrong.

Although I'd never planned to go into the family business, I didn't know what else I wanted to do. When the small marine-procurement company I worked for went into receivership, my dad asked me to work for him. My first job was to be a quality auditor, but I ended up taking on the role of health and safety in the factory too. This was a difficult job. Not only was I the boss's son – a position that's generally hated by the rest of the workforce – but also, I was in charge of health and safety, an equally hated role.

To the lads on the shop floor and the management team, this "new-fangled European law", as the production manager called it, was just a distraction from getting the products out of the door. They didn't seem to realise its importance, and back then far less emphasis was placed on health and safety.

Like most manufacturing businesses, the factory had its ups and downs, but by the time I started working for my dad back in 2000 had been running for more than thirty years, it had a great local reputation and it had some good contracts with big companies.

From a systemisation point of view, the business was better than most but it still wasn't good enough to escape what was coming. It had a reasonable management structure in place, although some of the managers wouldn't be up to task by today's standards. It was certified by the International Organization for Standardization (ISO), which meant that everything had an audit trail. ISO certification states that every person has a role and that there is a process for everything. In theory, it means the company is accountable from a personal and manufacturing perspective. In other words, if there's a problem with a product you can go through the entire process to see who made it, when, using what material and how was it checked.

Having ISO certification is a good start, but to be truly systemised you need to take it one step further, as I will explain in this book. The consultancy firm that came into my father's business wrote a manual based on how they were told the company operated and then they left. They didn't make any improvements or suggestions, and this turned out to be a huge problem.

Then my father, the lynchpin of the business, died and the business – and our livelihoods – died with him.

Why systemise?

Before we look at how to systemise a business, we need to understand why. Is it worth the effort and expense? How quickly will we see a benefit? Can we afford it? I believe the benefits outweigh the one disadvantage, which is that it takes time to get everything running efficiently and effectively. So, instead of asking "Why systemise?" we should be asking "Why shouldn't I systemise?" The guidance in this book will help you systemise your business more quickly and save you making the same mistakes that I did.

A letting agent once asked me for advice. He said he was being a busy fool. He was doing all the viewings, the accounts, the cleaning – everything. So, I explained what I had done to systemise my company and how this freed me up to work *on* the business rather than *in* the business, driving it forward. I went through all the systems and how they would help him. He replied that he didn't have time to write a manual, train employees and so on. I couldn't believe what I was hearing! I had explained the huge benefits of turning his business around, but he couldn't find the time to put it into practice. A year later, I bumped into him again and we chatted about his business. He told me that the only things that had changed were that he was even busier and was working even longer hours.

If you want to change in your business, your attitude is a great place to start.

Better individual performance

If employees are certain about their responsibilities, it stands to reason that their performance will improve. Think of it in sporting terms: a rugby team has several players with completely different roles. The winger doesn't get involved in the scrum, and the prop isn't going to be kicking the penalties. These rules allow each member of the team to perform the same role again and again, which helps them become more efficient in that role. Why do you think Usain Bolt is good at running the 100 metres? Because he practises it over and over again. He doesn't compete in the high jump or the marathon: he trains hard to become the best he can be in one event. He has systemised his actions and repeated them numerous times to become the best at what he does.

It's the same with procedures. If you know your role well and you do it every day, you will become better at it and your performance will improve. We like rules – we like to know what's expected of us. In Charles Duhigg's excellent book *The Power of Habit*, he says, "Champions don't do extraordinary things. They do ordinary things, but they do them without thinking, too fast for the other team to react. They follow the habits they've learned." In a business context, by doing the same procedural action over and over again we get better and better at it, which undoubtedly improves individual performance.

Better company performance

When the vast majority of employees are performing well in their individual roles, it's impossible for the company not to improve. When audits all come back with small or minor necessary changes or amendments and individual learning objectives are being met, the company as a whole will improve. Although many people see companies as static beasts, if run correctly they can be organic and their health gets better or worse based on the sum of their parts and their performance.

Many of the awards that we work hard to achieve in business are down to the systems we have. In my case, the *Sunday Times* awards, Investors in People, my personal accolades, *Sunday Times* outstanding contribution to lettings (I'm on the board of directors for the Association of Residential Letting Agents – ARLA) and appointments are all thanks to making the time to commit to new challenges and opportunities. This wouldn't have been possible without good systems.

Increased profit

We all work in business to make money. The social responsibility side of my business, where we fund and help to train some of our tenants, wouldn't be possible without the profit that the commercial makes. With a well-oiled, systemised company, you'll make more money in the following ways.

- **Efficiency savings.** Systemising your business will improve the way you currently operate and you will become slicker.
- **Effectiveness.** Systemising will allow you to have a better impact.
- **Being able to see where you are losing money.** We have consulted with more than one hundred other businesses and they have all admitted that they were wasting money in areas where they hadn't known they were losing it. Systems show you where this is happening.

Motivated staff

It's worth systemising your business for this reason alone. People are motivated by competent colleagues. When we work with good people, our job is much easier and being at work is, dare I say it, enjoyable. If a member of staff is not at work, systems make sure that somebody else can do that person's job so it doesn't hold the business up.

For example, in a buddy system, if someone is off then their "buddy" answers their urgent emails and enquiries in their absence. This means problems can be solved when employees are away from work, and people returning don't come back to major issues. Most importantly, the customer doesn't have to wait, as they can speak to someone who understands their situation and is often able to answer their query there and then. Give staff better colleagues and watch their motivation increase.

More options

As I found out when I lost my dad, time is the only commodity we can never get enough of, so it's important to use it wisely. No one ever said on their deathbed that they wished they'd spent more time at work – it's always, "I wish I'd spent more time with my family", "I wish I'd done more of the things I wanted to do" or "I wish I'd travelled more". Having a business that can function without you so that you can do the things you love should be your ultimate goal.

There's a huge difference between being self-employed or working for yourself (that is, you *are* the business) and owning a business. It doesn't matter how large the turnover is or how many people you employ – the main deciding factor in whether you own a business or not how much it relies on you, the owner.

Imagine you've taken three months off to travel round the world. If you come back and the bills haven't been paid and the jobs haven't been processed, no matter what the size of the "business" you are actually self-employed. There's nothing wrong with being self-employed, as long as you recognise that and act accordingly. If you come back after your three-month trip and the business is running well (or, in my case, I'm told it runs better without me) you truly do have a business.

Scale up and grow

To quote Michael Gerber in *The E-Myth Revisited*, "How is it that McDonald's can deliver on its customer promise in every one of its 20K plus restaurants, each and every day, when a small business owner can't do it with a single location?" Businesses fail to grow for many reasons. Cash-flow is the main issue, but another common reason is that the success of the first branch was down to the owner's interpersonal skills. Unless you can replicate that person, any new branches won't provide the same level of business or customer service as the original branch.

Systems help us set out in a structured format the things that make that person unique and duplicate them in another branch so there are fewer chances of failure each and every time. Returning to the McDonald's example, the reason we know that a hamburger bought in London, Tokyo or Los Angeles will taste the same is down to the systems that McDonald's is famous for. These systems give the customer a consistent experience and are an important reason for the rapid growth of the company.

If you want the big business empire, you won't achieve it without systems. They are integral to the scaling and growing of your business.

A saleable asset

Anyone who's bought or sold a business will know that a big part of its value or risk is its senior management team. I've bought ten businesses and sold a couple. Within a matter of months, sometimes weeks, it was possible to increase the income and decrease the costs. This is partly thanks to the structures and systems I have put in place, but it's also down to how the target company is set up.

Each of these businesses lacked systems. Most didn't even have financial indicators or the ability to measure their performance. In most cases, the person who owned the business *was* the business – everything relied on them. This meant I could make a lower offer, as inevitably my company would lose a small proportion of business that was based on clients' personal relationship with the previous owner.

A few years ago, I noticed that a small agency was for sale in Sunderland. One of the big national chains was selling it, as the agency didn't fit the chain's profile any more. When I spoke to the sales and acquisitions director I knew in the first thirty seconds that we couldn't do a deal, as they wanted more than I was prepared to offer, but we continued to talk about business. She then gave me a golden nugget of information: she said that if a company was not systemised they would offer around six or seven times the net profit but if it was systemised, they would offer up to twelve times the net profit, as long as the owner wasn't integral to the business. It was one of those eureka moments – I realised that if I ever wanted to sell my business, to get the best price I would have to systemise it so much that I made myself redundant.

Any larger company with its eyes on your company will want to know it is run correctly. They'll want to know that it would still perform to the same financial level if they bought your company and you decided to leave.

As well as commanding a much higher sale price for being systemised, you'll have more potential buyers. Sometimes, a buyer will offer a lower amount or a highly deferred payment at the last minute. If that's your only potential buyer, you'll be more likely to take the reduced amount. But if you have several buyers lined up, as most smoothly operated businesses do, you can refuse the offer without losing a sale altogether or you can tell the potential buyer that you have a few interested parties.

In John Warrillow's book *Built to Sell: Creating a Business That Can Thrive Without You*, he states that it's important not to be synonymous with your business. If buyers aren't confident that the business can run without you, they won't make you the best offer. Warrillow also emphasises that by *being* the business you are severely limiting your choice of buyers.

How systemising worked for me

As you can imagine, the time following my dad's death was pretty tough.

After the company went into receivership, I got a job as a health and safety officer at Jennings Winch and Foundry in Sunderland. While working there I moved house and stumbled upon an old business plan that I had written with my dad about buying a few properties. Having lost the family business, I decided to revisit the plan with a view to buying some property as a pension.

First, I updated the plan and made it more detailed. I then re-mortgaged my home and bought three properties using the money I'd released as deposit. This was in the days when you only needed a 15% deposit to purchase buy to let properties and the value of property was increasing rapidly. I managed to build a portfolio of fifteen properties fairly quickly. In August 2008, I set up Castledene

Property Management to manage my portfolio and that of other landlords.

However, I had substituted a job for a job. I was working long hours doing tasks that didn't bring in any money. I'd never employed people before, and when I look back at my recruitment process, it was embarrassing. My initial recruitment policy wasn't far from asking the candidate if they liked property and then, depending on their answer, offering them a job!

Reading *The E-Myth* by Michael Gerber opened my eyes to how we'd been operating – we'd been firefighting, we hadn't been employing great staff, and we'd been performing poorly on customer service, which isn't easy to admit as a business owner. Gerber's book helped me understand the importance of processes and systems for improving the business and getting the work-life balance I needed to work efficiently.

I wrote the first systems for my business in a crude and basic way. In two months, I came up with a basic twenty-page manual that set out roles and responsibilities, which made people accountable. I often used to hear, "Oh, I thought that was their job" or "I didn't know I had to do that". The manual stopped all that and allowed my company to become much more settled.

As the company grew, so did the systems. I soon realised that the operations manual was just the beginning. To truly systemise a business is a much bigger process and is far more difficult. Today, the systems allow employees to reach their potential and be efficient, and new branches to be integrated into the group structure.

Due to this rapid improvement, my business started to get recognised in the industry. In the *Sunday Times* Letting Agency of the Year Awards, which are the industry equivalent of the Oscars, we've won national awards every year since 2012, which is a huge achievement.

Overview of the systemisation framework

The five-part systemisation framework includes the following steps:

1. Writing your operations manual
2. Training your staff
3. Auditing your processes
4. Giving effective feedback on the audit
5. Reviewing your process.

These five things can make the difference between success and failure, good and great companies, and making a profit or losing money. It sounds simple, but as my father used to say, "If it was that obvious, son, everyone would be doing it". Guess what ... they're not.

In the following chapters I break down each of the five parts of the framework, that I have come up with, using layman's terms and giving examples. I've included several real examples from my award-winning systems manual and training programmes to help you get started. You can adapt these to suit you and your business. I've also included forms for collecting audit data.

I often get asked why I want to give away the company secrets and whether I'm worried that our customers will go elsewhere if our competitors get their hands on our systems. I'll answer by telling a story.

When I first went to the USA to train in mixed martial arts, I trained with the then Ultimate Fighting Championship (UFC) light heavyweight title-holder, Randy Couture. During our training sessions I asked him many questions about diet, training, fitness and mind-set and he openly told me all the tips and tricks that had got him to the top of his game. When I asked him why he was telling me all this, he said that nothing he knew was a secret. All the wrestling tips he had given me were available from any high-school wrestling coach, all the diet advice was available on the internet, and even the mind-set tools could be found in any good book. But I'll never forget what he said next: "You will never work as hard as me to achieve what I have achieved." At first, I thought that was presumptuous and arrogant, but then I realised he was right. After all, he was the UFC champion and lived in the USA where all the best trainers, coaches and fighters were. I lived in a small town in England with a young daughter who I wouldn't have left to take up a place over there.

The moral of the story is that even though this book explains what you need to do, you might not put it into practice. You must *want* to systemise your business and give it everything you have.

It will be hard work. If you employ staff, some will fight against the changes you make and question why you are making them. Some people will not make the journey with you, so be prepared for that. I lost 25% of my employees in the first eight months of systemising the business. This gave us the opportunity to employ people who "got it", and most of them are still with us today.

Keep going back and reviewing each process set out in this book until you understand them fully. Never implement anything in your business without understanding it or being fully committed. This needs to be a business change, and you need commitment to make it to work. It's no good trying it for a few weeks and then giving up. Your staff won't respect you for it and your business will suffer. As the saying goes, decide, commit, succeed.

Company-defining documents

Before we can unleash ourselves on the five-part system, we need to design and agree on what I call the company-defining documents. These documents set the tone for how you run your business, how you work as an individual and how your employees engage with you. It's a bold claim, but if you get this right it will make everything else much easier.

These documents are an essential foundation for systemising your business. You will not get the best out of your business without them. If you have a bad night's sleep and go to the gym feeling tired and stressed, you're not going to have the best training session because your mind isn't focused. These documents will get you focused so you can achieve your best.

Company core values

These are the identity of a company – the defining factor that gives your company the edge over a competitor. They are the beliefs or philosophy of the company.

Your core values and beliefs will define what you include in your operations manual. Writing a manual is easy – anyone can do it. But writing a manual that ensures you provide exceptional customer service makes the difference between being an OK company and being an exceptional company.

- Core values tell your customers what your company is about. Think of them as your competitive advantage, not a burden.
- Core values help you recruit and retain staff. For perfect synergy between staff and company, all your values need to be aligned.

- Core values form part of your decision-making process. Even when you have to make a difficult decision, if you make it with your core values in mind, people will respect you for sticking to the company beliefs.

In his article "Aligning action and values", Jim Collins says: "First, you cannot 'set' organisational values, you can only discover them. Nor can you 'install' new core values into people. Core values are not something people 'buy in' to. People must be predisposed to holding them." I entirely agree, and this is why you need to discover what your core values are at the earliest opportunity.

If you already employ people, this process might be a bit trickier – when you discover your company core values, you may find that you employee people who don't align with them. Remember, some employees will not make the journey with you, but this is the small price to pay for a systemised business. Jim Collins goes on to use an analogy he calls the "Mars Group". He asks: if you could pick only five people to send to Mars to shout about your company, who would you send? Those five people will be the ones who have a gut instinct for your values without being told them.

Your values should stay the same regardless of how many different businesses you are in. If you sold your company tomorrow and bought another one the next day, your values shouldn't change. They are what is important to you. Core values are innate part of your character. As the famous American basketball coach John

Wooden said, "The true test of a man's character is what he does when no one is looking".

One of Disney's core values is "Dream" while 3M's is "Innovation". Those words sum up the two companies perfectly. What words define you and your company? How would you want your company to be described? What does it stand for? And what higher purpose do you want all of your employees to buy into?

Mission statement

A mission statement is a company's core aim set out in writing. Usually, it doesn't change over time. At a basic level, your mission statement sets out what you do and why you do it.

A good mission statement:

- Acts as a filter that separates what is important from what is not
- Clearly states which markets you serve and how
- Communicates a sense of intended direction to the entire company.

A well-defined and meaningful mission statement is a great tool for understanding and communicating your business objectives to staff. It should be expressed in only a sentence or two.

Like your company core values, your mission statement is part of the foundations for your business and the main rules that employees should follow. These are not the specific rules of a football game that are written down in law, these are the more cultural values, such as shaking hands after a game and clapping the opposing team off or not taking a hard, but fair, tackle personal. These define a person and the business.

When recruiting, we explain our mission statement to candidates, because we want to employ people who share our vision, values and beliefs.

You need to answer three questions when writing your mission statement:

1. What do we do?
2. Who do we do it for?
3. What value do we bring?

Here are some examples of great mission statements:

"To refresh the world, to inspire moments of optimism and happiness through our brands and actions, to create value and create a difference."
Coca-Cola

"To organize the world's information, and make it universally accessible and useful."
Google

"We seek to be the Earth's most customer-centric company, for four primary customer sets consumers, sellers, enterprisers and content creators"
Amazon

"To bring inspiration and innovation to every athlete in the world."
Nike

"To attract and attain customers, with high-valued products and services and the most satisfying ownership experience in America."
Toyota

Use the above and others mission statements as inspiration but, as with the core values, you need to find your own mission statement that you believe in 100%. If you don't believe in your mission statement, your lack of passion will show.

Simon Sinek said, "Customers will never love a company unless the employees love it first". Coming up with the right values and mission statement is a great start.

RECAP

In this chapter, you've learned:

- Bad things happen for no good reason – it might happen to you, so it's important to bullet-proof yourself and your business.
- Systems help to:
  - Improve individual performance
  - Improve company performance
  - Maximise profit

- Increase staff motivation
- Give you options
- Scale up and grow
- Give you a saleable asset.
- Company-defining documents are:
    - Company core values
        - Tell your staff and customers what you are all about
        - Help recruit and retain staff
        - Form part of the decision-making process.
    - Mission statement
        - Tells people what you do
        - Tells people who you do this for
        - Communicates the value you bring.

Tasks

- Write your own company values. Remember, make sure they are *your* values, not the values that you think people will want you to have.

- Write your own mission statement. Use others for guidance and inspiration, but make sure you own your mission statement.

ONE
THE OPERATIONS MANUAL
A List Of Rules

Many people think that you can systemise a business simply by writing a manual. Nothing could be further from the truth. The manual is the basis for the systemisation process, but it's only 20% of the process. Having said that, it is the part that takes the longest to get right. You need to get it as complete as you can, right from the start.

The operations manual is like the cornerstone of a building or the engine of a car. Without it, the rest of the process is a waste of time and energy. When I wrote our first operations manual all those years ago, I was jumping for joy. It was my first step to business freedom. Even though it was only twenty pages long and full of spelling mistakes, it showed me I was heading in the right direction.

When writing your operations manual, be aware that you won't get it right first time. It's a huge step in the right direction, but some of your employees won't thank you for it. Persistence and consistency are the keys here. If employees show resistance and pick holes in your manual, that's to be expected. It happened to me and it has happened to everyone who's consulted us.

People don't like change. It's a natural feeling, especially for long-serving staff. We shouldn't be surprised if they are wary of the operations manual. They might worry that the aim of the manual is to make them redundant. In fact, nothing is further from the truth – the only person it aims to make redundant is you.

Remember, not everyone will make the journey with you. This move towards systemising your business may polarise opinion. Some people will thrive on it and it will be the change they were waiting for. Others will resent it and will look for other jobs, as their performance can now be measured, highlighted and managed accordingly. These are the ones who might not have been performing to the best of their ability while you and your other employees have been slogging your guts out, blissfully unaware that you've been covering for them.

At this point, I also need to mention those of us who employ good friends, partners or family. Introducing changes may lead to arguments in your personal life. As we all know, working with people who we have a relationship with outside work can be difficult. Separating the two worlds is impossible for some people. The question you need to ask is this: Does my personal relationship with these people mean more to me than my business and my family's future? If the answer is yes, you don't need to read any more of this book, as systemising your business is not for you. But if you want great company performance, a saleable asset and the option to retire, and you want to bring those family and friends along with you, carry on reading.

As with most things, it's not what you say – it's how you say it. Telling your staff what you intend to do and how you're going about it can make all the difference. If you say, "I'm systemising the business, so it's my way or the highway", you should expect friction and anger. But if you're genuine and explain that the manual is there to help everyone, to make their jobs easier and more efficient and to benefit the customer, you'll get a better response.

Plan what you are going to say to your employees. Never just send an e-mail – it's impersonal and it doesn't give people the chance to ask questions.

Make sure everyone understands what's going to happen. Communicate with them at every point along the way. Business decisions that demand co-operation from staff at all levels deserve nothing less than effective communication.

What is the operations manual?

The operations manual is the company bible. We call ours the Castledene Way, and if something isn't in the Castledene Way, we don't do it. So, your manual needs to set out everything about your business, from how to operate machinery, to how you interact with customers, to how you report your results, to what you do when things go wrong. If something happens in your business that isn't in your manual, your manual is not complete.

Going back to the car analogy, you could have the best car in the world on your drive (the Aston Martin DB7, by the way), but if it's missing a front tyre, it's just a piece of metal. It isn't fit for the purpose it was designed for. This is the same as not having a complete operations manual. If there are gaps, according to Murphy's law, whatever can go wrong will go wrong.

We don't like mistakes – we want things to be perfect as quickly as possible. But perfection takes time. If you're going to systemise your business, you need to be prepared to put in the hours at the beginning to reap the rewards at the end. I assure you, it's worth it.

So, should your procedures simply detail what you do? Of course not – because what you do might not be the best way of doing it. If you already have a business, you need to go back to basics. If you're just starting one, this is even better, as you haven't got into the habit of running your business in a certain way.

As the saying goes, you need to work *on* your business rather than *in* it. Imagine looking down on your business as if you're looking down on a patient on the operating table. Sometimes you won't like what you see, but brutal honesty is your friend. Anything less is not doing you, your staff, your business or your customers any favours.

Take another analogy: I love my children with all my heart, but I don't look at them through rose-tinted glasses. If they mess up, I tell them. If they're naughty, I don't pacify them with a treat. To prepare them for the real world, I treat them with honesty. This is how you need to look at the current way you run your business.

If things aren't working well in a particular part of the business, recognise that. If certain members of staff aren't pulling their weight, that needs to be specifically identified and addressed. The aim of the manual is to help you be the best you can be – anything less is cheating.

Although I've never met you and I don't know what you do, I know you're not running your business as efficiently or effectively as possible. How do I know this? It's simple – no business runs at 100% all the time. It's impossible. People don't perform, machinery breaks down and automation fails. It's how we deal with these issues that determines how successful we are.

When writing your manual, on the one hand you need to write down what you do, but on the other hand you need to ignore what you do. Confused? Let me explain.

First, take into account your company core values and your mission statement. These may be bold and ambitious, but remember, "go big or go home". These documents will keep you on the right track when you're writing your manual.

Second, write the manual with the end user in mind. By end user I don't mean your staff, who will be the ones reading, using and implementing the procedures. I mean the customer, who will use your product or service. Your values and beliefs will shine through in the procedures in your operations manual.

Everything in your manual must revolve round the customer. Now, I don't subscribe to the belief that the customer is always right, or even often right. Some people just like to moan, and you can't please everyone all the time. Not everyone likes Nike, Apple or Aston Martin, and these are three leading brands in their industries. I subscribe to Ken Blanchard's idea of having "raving fans" not customers. "Raving fans" are the people who receive such good customer service from you that they want to shout about how good you are. Our ordinary customers will just say, "Oh yes, I use Castledene to manage my properties", but our fans tell everybody at every opportunity. Because of them, we get a large number of referrals and repeat business.

Writing your operations manual is your opportunity to make your service better and more customer-focused. The broad brushstrokes of what you do may be the same, but by tweaking the details you can improve the service. Orienting your manual to customer service won't put an end to all complaints – remember, you can't please all the people all the time. So, write your manual with the majority in mind.

Never be tempted to fit the procedures in your operations manual around your staff. I have seen businesses make this mistake countless times. Never compromise on customer service because of a staffing inefficiency or an employee's lack of knowledge. Instead, invest time and effort in training or move employees around so everything's covered. Do you think your customer cares that Robert only works three days a week or Mary doesn't know how to use the software? Of course not, so don't put yourself or your business in that position.

Your operations manual is your chance to make your business super-efficient, but remember that it has to be realistic. It's no good writing procedures that you have no chance of following. Remember, superior customer service is the key!

The art of delegation - make yourself redundant

When writing your operations manual, your ultimate goal is to make yourself redundant. This might seem alien if you've worked hard for years and you're proud to have done so. But this is a unique situation. You need to make it possible for the business to operate as efficiently as possible without you. Remember when we went through the reasons to systemise? One that I think is most important is that systemising your business gives you a saleable asset.

You might never sell your business or pass it on to your children, but at least you'll have the option to do so if you wish. The most important of all the reasons to systemise is that it gives you more options – options to spend more time with your family and make sure they never have to go through anything like mine did when we lost my dad.

The excuses

There are two types of people in the world – those who do things and the ones who make excuses. Believe me, I've heard them all from people I've worked with. Ultimately, whether you delegate is down to you and your desire to change your life.

No one can do it as well as I can.

If this is your excuse, either you have too high an opinion of yourself or your employees are not up to the task. If the problem is your staff, you have two options. You can either invest time and effort in upskilling people so they can perform the tasks to the required standard or you can recruit people who are better skilled and more competent.

I know I'm not the best person at my job – and if I can accept that, you can too. That means there are people out there who you can subcontract to or delegate to. What's important is to be able to see people's potential and let go.

I just don't have the time to train the staff.

The brutally honest answer to this excuse is that you need to make time. You can't do anything worthwhile overnight – it takes hard work, dedication and persistence. So if you want to achieve the end goal you need to put the hard graft in. We will go over some tips on how to break down the training process later.

Who can I delegate to?

The first question you need to ask yourself is whether a task should be delegated internally or externally. Here's how this worked for me.

When I started the company, I did everything myself: the accounts, the viewings, meeting the landlords, the internal paperwork and much more. I had two members of staff who worked hard and did what I asked of them, but without good systems there was no real consistency and stability.

So, when I first systemised the business, I looked at all the jobs I was doing and identified which income-generating tasks I could delegate internally or externally. I was surprised by how many tasks I could easily pass to someone else.

I delegated the accounts to a local accountant, who not only did a much better job than I could but also made the process of recording invoices and receipts much more efficient. It paid for itself from day one, as I was spending no time at all on accounts.

Remember, your time has value, so value it. I managed to delegate the viewings to one member of staff, who thrived on it and again did a brilliant job. I also employed an additional person to manage a portfolio of properties that I had been managing. This freed up huge amounts of my time.

I enjoyed and was good at getting business in, so I continued to do that. As soon as my workload increased and resources allowed, I delegated more tasks to free up more of my time to continue working on income-generating tasks.

After a few years, I was in the position where almost any task in the business could be delegated to internal employees. This includes training, audits, human resources, setting targets and recruitment. I don't get involved in anything to do with running the business. I could retire tomorrow if I wanted to, but I love what I do and I still have a passion for growing the business.

Look at each task. Can you give it to someone internally? With the right training, are they capable of completing the task to the company's high standard? Or can you delegate it, like I did with the accounting, to an external professional?

There's a cost involved in delegating, and I appreciate that when you're starting out things can be tight in the finance department. Having said that, the time and effort you'll save by delegating also has a cost implication, as you'll be free to perform the tasks that bring in the income.

When I first bought properties, I refurbished them myself because I thought it would save time and money. I did save money on each particular job, but overall it was a terrible decision for the business. I missed out on countless deals with estate agents because I was too busy stripping wallpaper or knocking down walls. Eventually I learned that getting someone else in to do the work not only resulted in a better standard of refurbishment but also freed me up to look for the next deal and visit the estate agents.

It's a false economy to think you'll save money by doing everything yourself. In the long run, you'll miss out on opportunities that could have made you much more money.

Whether you can delegate enough tasks to make yourself redundant in the business will depend on where you are in the business process. If you're just starting out, you may have to do many of the tasks yourself and delegating might not always be possible. But it's still important to take a long, hard look at all the tasks you're doing to see if you really do have to do them yourself or if you can pass them to someone else, not necessarily in the business.

As explained above, holding on to tasks is counterproductive. It's better to let other people do the tasks that don't make you money or are time-consuming and laborious. This leaves you to push the business forward.

Delegation is an art, not a science. It takes time to let go. You need the right people in the right areas of the business, supporting you in the right way. You also need people who buy in to your business vision and beliefs. Have frank conversations with people you want to delegate to – especially if they don't work directly for you, as you'll have less control over how they represent your business. Don't see this as a reason not to work with them. Instead, use it as a starting point for the conversation. Explain what you need from them and set the expectations from the beginning. Delegate at the earliest opportunity.

> **TOP TIP** Write a list of everything you do including the amount of time it takes you to carry out that particular action. Next to each item, write the name of someone in the business who could take on this task or someone it could be delegated to externally. Ensure the people you want to delegate to have the skills or the resources to upskill themselves so they can take on the additional tasks successfully. You will be surprised at how much you can delegate.

Breaking down your operations manual into procedures

The operations manual is the business bible, but it will be broken down into bite-sized procedures. These are sometimes called standard operating procedures (SOPs) or working procedures. In this book, we'll keep it simple and call them procedures.

Your procedures need to be clear and simple enough for everyone to understand and follow. Don't use complicated language and don't include actions that are too difficult to follow. We lovingly refer to our procedures as "the idiot's guide", because we want anyone to be able to follow them without needing someone else to explain them. A good test is to ask someone not connected to the business to read through your procedures. My better half Gemma got this particular job. She spent many an evening going through them at the dining room table, telling me either that a procedure didn't make sense or that she understood it perfectly.

Who should write the procedures?

This depends on what stage you're at in your business. I suggest that you write them yourself until you have the right staff in place to write them for you, but as soon as you employ people who can write the procedures, get them to do it, thus making yourself even more redundant.

I know somebody who owns an estate agency who asked one of his employees to write the operations manual. He said he didn't have the time to do it himself, which usually means, "I say I want it but I don't want to put in the hard work". The employee wrote the manual with the best intentions at heart, but within a few months they had a legal case on their hands because she hadn't considered the law when writing the eviction procedure. He made the time after that!

I wrote all my business's procedures for the first few years, partly because I enjoyed doing it and partly because the property industry has a lot of legislation to comply with. Once I got to the stage when I employed people who were knowledgeable about the legal aspects of the industry, I delegated writing the procedures. At first it was difficult to give up control, but I needed to do this if I wanted to make myself redundant.

So, until you have the right staff, you need to write your procedures. But you still need to consult people within your company, regardless of its size or how many people you employ. The larger the business, the less you will know about or be able to control on a micro scale. That's just a part of business life. You can't know about everything that goes on in a business when it grows.

If you delegate writing the procedures to other people, I suggest you look over them until you are confident that your employees know how to write them and buy in to the company values and beliefs.

My managing director, Adele, is better at writing our procedures than I was. Because she has worked her way up, she understands the inner workings of the company and the software that we use. I'm completely fine with this – as I have a different role within the business.

A procedure for procedures

In Sam Carpenter's book *Work the System* he mentions creating a procedure for procedures. It sounds a little like something from *Alice in Wonderland*, but it's true. You need a working procedure for how you write your procedures. This is because at some point, you won't be writing the procedures any more so someone else needs to have written instructions on how to document a procedure. If you are repeatedly needed to write the procedures, you are not truly redundant and you don't have the right staff. Remember, you want to get to a point where you have nothing to do with recruitment, finances, auditing, training and development or writing procedures.

Mapping your procedures

We've looked at the basics and the theory about procedures, but how do you start writing them? This is the most common question I am asked about operating procedures. It seems to be such a daunting task. To be honest, it's not that difficult. As with anything worthwhile, it just takes time.

So how do we order the procedures and break them down? This is a perfect example of the saying, "Eat the elephant one bite at a time". Our operations manual is now over 330 pages long, but process-mapping helped us break this huge task down and make it easier.

A process map is a visual way of making a process much easier to understand and showing how it fits into the overall business strategy. Put simply, mapping a process entails drawing a box for each procedure and connecting the boxes to show the flow of work. Once you've done this, you can start to describe the individual processes in more detail.

Before writing the manual, you need to plan it meticulously. If you leave a procedure out it will make more work for you when you have to come back and include it. The initial effort should go into coming up with a list of all the procedures in the business, without worrying about the detail. Don't begin with the first procedure and attempt to write it from start to finish. Think of this list as the index or contents of a book. It's a list of all the procedures in the operations manual. We list our procedures in a chronological order, as from the first time we come into contact with the customer and how that interaction flows from action to action. The actions logically flow in a certain order and we make sure the procedures do too.

After making your list, and you're happy with it, you need to start at the beginning and map each procedure, writing it as you go. Always map the procedure before writing it.

As the purpose of this book is to make systemisation simple and easy for small- to medium-sized enterprises, I won't be discussing more complicated process-mapping tools, such as the Enterprise business process model and Dr Geary Rummler's super system model. These can be too complex for non-corporate or project management individuals.

I know a successful businesswoman in property who spent a small fortune on hiring somebody to put her systems and processes in place. The guy was really well qualified and came up with some great systems, but they were far too complicated for her staff, who struggled immensely with them. Always write the procedures so your staff can understand them.

When designing the initial process map for each procedure in your operations manual, use the symbols shown below. These show you at a glance what to expect within the procedure. The start and end symbols indicate the first and last parts of the process. Rectangular boxes show steps in the process and diamonds show decisions that need to be made (either/or, yes/no, left/right, etc.). Circles containing a letter or letters are page connectors. If a process spills onto another page, two page connectors with the same letter are attached to the last process step on the first page and the first process step on the next page. Databases and physical documents are indicated as shown.

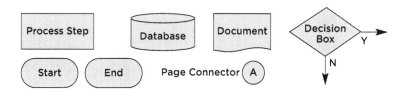

Edward Zunich, who has written several great books on Practical Process Improvement, states that to get the best out of your process map, you need to take the 30,000 foot view. Imagine you are in a plane cruising at 30,000 feet and you're looking at the ground below. You can only see the general topography, not the detail. This allows you to focus on the big picture – the roads, larger buildings and so on – without worrying about the smaller parts.

Rather than complicate things by talking about processes in a specific industry, let's process-map a simple task that we can all relate to: making toast. No matter how simple or complex the process, it can still be mapped.

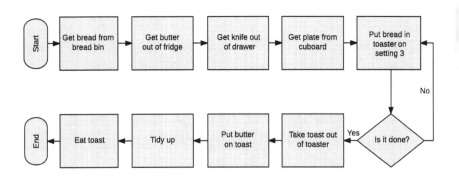

See how easy it is to process-map something like making toast. This is more than good enough for the initial process-mapping in your operations manual. All you need to do now is apply this to each procedure in your business. It will take time and you won't get it right straight away, but stick at it – it will be worth it.

> **TOP TIP** Use Post-it notes on a whiteboard or a wall. If you're not sure what order some of the business processes follow, you can easily switch round the Post-it notes.

Ordering your procedures

When you process-map your business, make sure you start with the first thing people do. For example, we have "Castledene: the Basics" in which we explain what we expect of employees who work for us. Next, we have procedures for taking on a property, then for marketing that property, then for carrying out a viewing, then for taking an application, and so on. This provides a natural progression from taking on a property right through to selling it and everything in between. The process has to be logical and simple and have a natural flow. No, I haven't turned into a hippy: by natural flow, I mean that the manual must flow logically from process to process for it to make sense as a whole.

When listing processes in the order they naturally take place in your business, leave no stone unturned. It doesn't matter how small or insignificant a process might seem. If it is used in your business and it needs documenting, include it. For example, our feedback process is shorter than others and seems like common sense: at the end of the working day, we give feedback to the office. Obvious, right? But common sense isn't always common practice, so it needs to be documented.

Writing your procedures

So, you've process-mapped your procedures with all the main functions that need to be carried out. Now it's time to write the procedures, including all the detail you need for staff to understand and follow the procedure and provide great customer service. You can do this by using SMART thinking and by being PURE.

SMART thinking is a common concept in business. It's a great reminder that effective management doesn't need to be complicated.

Specific. This is an undervalued attribute of a written procedure. I have read procedures that are so open-ended and vague that you have no idea who is meant to be doing what. The whole idea of being specific is to nail down any potential gaps in the procedure.

To combat the most commonly used excuse when something goes wrong in a business – "Oh, I didn't know it was my job to do that" – set out who is responsible for carrying out a certain action. This may include more than one person and more than one action.

Note down all the people who are needed for the actions to be carried out and completed.

Don't note down the person's name; instead, use their job role (for example, accompanied viewer or branch manager). People will come and go more often than job roles change, so you won't have to update the procedures as often if you use job titles.

Being specific makes a huge difference when you're auditing the business and when you're dealing with complaints. If a procedure sets out clearly who is meant to do what, if an action isn't carried out the issue is easier to manage.

Measurable. I'm a huge fan of measuring my businesses, be that through key performance indicators (KPIs), metrics, financial controls or procedures. Write your procedures so that they can be measured. You can do this by providing a timeframe for completing a certain action or a standard that has to be reached. Always make sure you can measure the performance of your staff against what's included in the procedures.

Having great procedures makes staff performance easier to manage. A good business communicates with staff regularly through effective one-to-ones or other channels. Being able to measure employees' performance through procedures and communicating this to them will only help your business.

Agreed upon. Is your procedure agreed upon by all the stakeholders in the business? Since you are the business owner,

I'm presuming you agree with yourself, but what if someone else is writing the procedures in for you?

In my case, my Managing Director writes our procedures, or at least proofs them before they are implemented. Over the years we have worked closely and we share the same vision and strategy for the business, so I trust her judgement on how the procedures are written and what they aim to achieve.

This synergistic approach does take time. It doesn't happen overnight. Until people writing your procedures share your vision for the business, you should check the procedures to ensure you are all in agreement. Once you've achieved that, you can give people more freedom to write and implement the procedures.

It's a bit like letting your kids ride a bike. At first, you're an overbearing parent with your hands on the back of the saddle, nervous about letting go. But once you have confidence in their ability, you take your hands away and watch them ride. They might fall off a couple of times, but soon they won't need your help any more.

Realistic. Have you the capacity and resources to follow the procedures you have written? Again, this is based on common sense, but you'd be surprised by how many times I've read something that is unachievable or unrealistic.

I once read an operations manual for a small building contractor I was doing some consultancy work for. One of his procedures stated that the bricklayers had to lay a set number of bricks each day. It didn't take into account the weather, the dark winter nights, the type of bricks, the type of house or any other parameters. It just said "must lay X amount of bricks".

This was so unrealistic that it might as well not have been written in the first place. You want to keep staff feeling motivated, but giving them unrealistic procedures to follow is the quickest way to demotivate them. Keep things realistic and achievable.

Time-bound. Always include a timeframe if it is relevant to the procedure. Even if you have a specific and clear procedure, you need to include a deadline to avoid the excuses "I was going to do that tomorrow" and "I didn't know when I had to do it by".

When I started writing our procedures, people gave me all sorts of reasons why certain actions hadn't been done, and these were favourites of the staff I employed at the time. It's easy to fix, though, as it's as simple as putting a timeframe in. It might be "within forty-eight hours" or "by the first of the month", but make sure it's achievable. There's no need to give people two months to post a letter, but equally don't give them a day to write a 20,000-word report. Find a happy medium that keeps people motivated to keep striving.

The less well-known acronym PURE is equally important.

Positively stated. Don't make the procedures wishy-washy. Make sure they're to the point and written with intent so they can't be misconstrued. Using words like "must" and "need" also helps.

I've seen procedures that state "if you have the time" or "if resources allow". Although both these phrases may be true in that if you don't have the resources to carry out a process you can't achieve the end result, don't write them into the procedure as they provide reasons not to do the task.

Understood. The procedures need to be understood by everyone whose job role is mentioned. This links with the next chapter on training staff. When writing the procedures, make sure you think about who will be following them. Don't write at a high corporate level if the person who will need to follow the procedure has never worked in a corporate environment. Always write for the lowest common denominator so that everyone can read and understand the procedures.

Relevant. Write your procedures so they are relevant to the business and its overall goals. If the procedure is not relevant, remove it. When I started the business, we had more than fifty procedures. Even though it has grown massively since then, we've reduced our procedures to forty. Be brutally honest about which procedures you don't need, which you can make more relevant to the business and which you can merge.

Ethical. It goes without saying that everything you do as a business needs to be legal and ethical. This is easier said than done. A former letting-agent client of mine wrote a manual that had at least a dozen clear breaches of legislation in the first six procedures.

As the procedures manual must be kept to at all times, it's important to ensure that staff and contractors are following the best possible advice and practice. It's your reputation and business on the line here.

If you're in doubt, do research until you are sure that everything contained in the manual is ethical and legal.

SMART and PURE thinking are nothing new, but they're not present in many operations manuals – or in how people run their businesses.

Getting it right at the beginning means far fewer problems further down the line. It will take you longer to write the procedures in this style and may take some getting used to, but time spent at this stage is time saved later on.

Forms and appendix

In your business, you will need to complete certain forms and give certain information to customers. For example, we are forever handing out or emailing application forms and information to tenants and landlords especially about compliance.

To make sure the same relevant and up-to-date information is given to the right person at the right time, you need to reference the forms in your procedures and include them in an appendix. So, if an application form needs to be handed out at a certain stage of a process, you should state this clearly in the procedures.

Number the forms so that when a procedure says "hand out form 7 (valuation form)" you can quickly turn to form 7, knowing that it is the current version of the valuation form.

Over time, the forms and their numbers will become so synonymous with the procedure that people will start referring to the forms by their numbers, not their titles. This signals that people understand the relationship between the procedures and the associated documents: they "get it".

Revision status

If you improve your procedures and associated documents on a regular basis, the revision status can become confusing. Always have a document list that shows the latest revision status. You can then update the revision status on the main index each time you change an associated document.

I've worked with a company where even though there were only ten employees, three of them were using slightly different versions of the same form. This was important, as one revision was necessary due to a change in legislation. Systemisation is about getting everyone working from the same documents so they can deliver the same exemplary customer service.

Index

At the beginning of each of our procedures, forms and appendixes, we have a list of current documents. This shows all the documents in order and the current revision status. Some are on the second or third revision, while others are on the tenth or eleventh. The index tells me which is the latest version. I can then cross-reference this against any documents in use at any time to check staff are using the right version.

If your business has many procedures, unless you're organised and have a master index for the various parts of your manual, it's easy to mistakenly use an old version of a procedure. Although most of the procedure might be the same, one small change could make all the difference.

TOP TIP when you update a procedure, destroy all copies of the previous revision. Whether you store your procedures on paper or electronically, make sure you keep only the most recent revision. Inform all managers and relevant staff that a revision has been made and new training will be needed.

Screenshots

If you use websites and software, you'll need to mention them in your procedures. Instead of having a software manual and a procedures manual, it's more effective to combine them in one manual. You won't be able to integrate every software function into the operations manual, but you can include the most important ones.

This will save time because people won't need to flick through two different manuals, trying to extract information from one while reading the other. Systems are meant to make your job easier.

Software changes regularly, so you might need to update the screenshots. This sounds labour-intensive, but usually it isn't. If you keep on top of the changes, it's easy to maintain the procedures with only slight adjustments. You can also delegate these sorts of changes to someone else.

Most people are visual learners, so the old saying that a picture paints a thousand words is still true today. Using a screenshot can give employees an immediate understanding of the process; for example, which button they should press or where they should enter information.

There is plenty of software (some you have a free trial) that can help with this, Snagit, Lightshot, Greenshot and Camtasia are just a few. You can also use the snipping tool, which is free with Windows, or the Print Screen key. Embed screenshots into your procedures documents and add arrows or red circles to highlight certain functions.

Learning objectives

A few years ago I was talking to a friend who owned a company that provided vocational training to students across the UK. He advised me to include learning objectives in my procedures.

Learning objectives are statements that tell the learner, in this case your employee, what they are about to learn. They act as a brief summary of the procedure, telling staff at a glance what to expect.

Creating learning objectives also helps with writing the procedures. By writing down the learning objectives at the beginning of the procedure, you set out what you want to achieve, create a plan to keep to, focusing your writing on the task at hand.

When you have many procedures and a business with many facets to it, focusing on the procedure at hand certainly helps.

Write the learning objectives in a positive and authoritative manner. For example:

- You will understand...
- You will be able to...
- You will have the knowledge to...

This gives a positive message that employees will have achieved a certain learning action by the end of reading the procedure.

We will discuss learning objectives in more detail in the next chapter, on training.

Adapt, evolve and change

Your operations manual will change regularly. If it doesn't, it may mean the following:

- There have been no changes in legislation or regulation in your industry that affect your business.
- You have not grown the business to accommodate any staff.
- You are still doing the same thing that you did five years ago.
- Your business is already the most efficient and effective it can possibly be.

If all the above are relevant to your business then you won't need to adapt your procedures – but I'm fairly certain this won't be the case, especially the last point

I'll go into more depth about reviewing procedures later, but it's worth saying here that you or your staff will need to tweak them at various stages of the business.

RECAP

In this chapter, you've learned the following:

- Why you need to write an operations manual.
- How it fits in with systemising the business.
- You need to make yourself redundant in the business.
- It's important to write procedures with superior customer service in mind.
- You write the procedures until you have the right staff to write them for you.
- How to write the procedures using SMART and PURE thinking.
- How to process-map your systems.
- How to create an index of procedures:
  - Write down all the procedures you will need in your business from end to end.
  - Think logically about how the process links together in your in your business.

- What is the customer journey from when they contact you to leaving you?
- How to write individual procedures:
  - Map out each procedure.
  - Don't forget SMART and PURE.
  - Write with the customer in mind.
  - Use screenshots if necessary.
  - Use learning objectives to help you write them.
  - Don't forget to adapt and evolve.

Task

- Write down a list of procedures in your business so you have a good understanding of all the processes.

- Once you have done this, go through each process of the business, using the above points as guidance.

- Just get started – don't procrastinate

TWO

TRAINING

Show Them How To
Follow The Rules

Training your staff is one of the most complex and difficult parts of any business. Hundreds of books have been written on the subject, each with the author's own slant on the latest trend or coaching technique. I've done plenty of research on this topic to find out what works for my business.

Believe me, I've made some mistakes in the way we train our employees. Some people don't think it looks good to admit that they got something wrong or that things didn't go as planned. But anyone who's been in business will know that starting and running your own company isn't easy, especially when you're dealing with people.

It would be doing you a disservice to claim that everything is wonderful and that I've never made a mistake. I've always learned more from making mistakes than when things have gone smoothly. There's nothing more satisfying that correcting a mistake and finding you made a good call.

When I started training my staff on systems it was a case, embarrassingly, of handing them the twenty-page document and saying, "learn this". Believe it or not, I was surprised when things went wrong and they hadn't read it. So, I had to do something about it, and this is where my passion for training and development grew from. Just dumping a manual on people and expecting them to read it is more common practice than you might think. What's worrying is when managers or business owners then blame their staff for not learning the material. It's a bit like a teacher handing you a textbook and then expecting you to pass your exam with flying colours – it's just not going to happen.

We all learn at different paces and training needs to be tailored to suit the individual. With teaching and learning, one size does not fit all. It never will do: we all have our own strong points and areas where we need further development.

I started researching different learning styles and tests that tell us what our own learning style is. I always thought I was an auditory learner – someone who learns best when they are told something – but a test showed me that in fact I'm a visual and kinaesthetic learner, which means I need to be shown something and allowed to be hands-on. Once I knew this, I realised why I never retained anything like as much information when I listed to an audio books as I did when I picked up a book to read.

As the saying goes, you can't help how you learn but you can help how you teach. We have to adapt the various training methods to suit the individual. I wanted to use a variety of learning applications that would give people the best chance to absorb the information. For learning material to be effective, it needs to be consistent with the overall learning objective of the training and development plan – that is, to allow employees to be the best that they can be.

As with any training and development in a business, you need to be fully committed to the process and ensure that it isn't a passing phase. For training to be effective, it needs to become part of the culture of the business. Everyone, from the managing director to the apprentices, needs to buy in to the company mantra of continual improvement.

Another thing to consider is motivation. What makes people want to come to work and perform to the best of their ability? Is it the money? Is it the promise of extra holidays? Is it to get away from the husband or the kids?

Motivation has a direct link to not only performance but also the ability to absorb training. Think about the last time someone spoke to you while you were watching TV. I bet you didn't listen to or understand everything they said. That's because you weren't fully motivated to listen to them so you didn't take in all the information. It's the same with training. Members of staff may turn up, but are they truly present and will they take in the information that is shared with them?

The theories on workplace motivation all come down to one thing, although there are many different ways to describe it. Most of us want to be the best we can be. Effective training gives us this opportunity. This leads to a more motivated workforce that performs better, higher levels of customer satisfaction and, eventually, more profit.

The theory

For the purposes of this book, I have simplified the academic theories, providing brief summaries. As you can see, they all point to the same thing.

Abraham Maslow, in his famous theory "Hierarchy of Needs", described a person's desire for self-fulfilment as "self-actualisation" – in other words, their desire to realise their potential. This will only be achieved through training and development.

David McClelland, in his Three Needs Theory, called it "achievement motivation", which is when a person wants to achieve realistic but challenging goals and advance in their job. People have a strong need for feedback on their achievement and progress, and they need a sense of accomplishment.

Fredrick Hertzberg's Motivator-Hygiene Theory also recognised that true motivational factors are achievement and advancement.

None of these researchers said that money was the primary goal. In fact, Hertzberg said, "Viewed within the context of the sequences of events, salary as a factor belongs more in the group that defines the job situation and is primarily a dissatisfier." In other words, money is not a motivator. When business owners think people are motivated by money, they throw money at them in the form of higher wages or big bonuses. Then they're surprised when their staff aren't motivated and don't perform.

Money is important – after all, you need it to pay the bills. But the best way to motivate your staff is to train and develop them so they feel a sense of achievement. Money is an enabler, not a motivator. By motivating staff you'll get better individual performance, which leads to better company performance. That's part of the systemisation mantra.

Which methods work?

The training system I use has evolved a great deal in only a few years. I started by giving staff a series of procedures to learn in their own time. Then, I read them out or stood in front of a PowerPoint presentation. Looking back, not only was it soul-destroying but also it gave poor results.

I have since found that the most effective method of training staff on systems is hands-on group involvement or group learning. In the context of systems training, that means reading through the procedures and asking learners to carry out the physical task so they remember it. As we all know, if we do something often enough we have a much higher chance of remembering it through repetition.

Most learners won't immediately understand why they have to carry out a certain action and they are not always aware of the bigger picture. Discussing the procedure and explaining why we do certain things and not others makes the process more real and understandable. It also makes people feel that they're a part of the process.

During training, members of staff may highlight gaps and make some excellent suggestions. We get them to discuss the procedures, as this gives them the chance to critically analyse ideas and translate them into their own words to make them their own.

It is possible to cater for the various learning styles by planning a range of activities that include several ways of presenting the information. Due to the nature of learning and the complex ways in which we retain information, there are several ways to do this. Asking people to make things, draw things or act out a process will engage the right-hand side of the brain, while asking learners to make lists or to create statistical prompts engages the left-hand side of the brain.

Role-play learning and activity-based groups are often powerful and effective learning tools because, by using feedback after the experience, they engage both sides of the brain and get better results. When people learn something in a new way, they know it intuitively and understand it intellectually.

People need to be coached in all aspects of their job, not just how to follow procedures. Once you have a robust training and development plan for all staff, monitor it closely against the individual goals of each employee and the strategic goals of the company. It might sound harsh, but if staff goals are not aligned with those of the company, your employees will not perform as you need them to and you will need to decide whether to keep them.

Individual training and development plans

I cannot emphasise enough the importance of having a training and development plan for each employee. This is critical to your company's success and ongoing development. Each employee plays a vital part in the evolution of a business. If someone doesn't seem to be essential, either they're the wrong employee or the role is not needed. All staff have a role to play, from the managing director, who is responsible for the strategic direction of the business, to the cleaning staff, who help maintain the brand image and keep the office a clean and hygienic place to work. As such, everyone's performance needs to be measured and improved as necessary.

Just for the record, I have an individual training and development plan. Why should I be any different from any other employee? I' have recently completed a Level 7 course in Leadership and management and am currently working on a Master's to take my learning even further.

I do this for a couple of good reasons. Firstly, every time I learn something interesting, I research it and, if applicable, implement it in the business. This has a positive effect on the business, so the company and our staff benefit. Secondly, because of the systemisation of the business, I am able to take on a time-consuming and, let's face it, difficult course. It's a great feeling to know that I have freed up enough time to learn about my passion and that what I learn will benefit the company. Learning is part of my job, and the information I learn will make everyone's lives easier and help us make more money.

Individual training and development plans provide several benefits.

Less management. Having fully trained and continuously developing staff means you have to spend less time managing them. Some companies believe they haven't got enough time to invest in staff development, but this is short-sighted. A well-trained team needs managing less, which saves everyone time.

Address employee weaknesses and improve customer service. Everyone you employ, including you, has a weakness in some area and this will have an impact on customer service. Finding out what the weaknesses are and adapting the training plan to address them will improve customer service. As mentioned earlier, it will also motivate your staff, as it will give them the opportunity to be better versions of themselves. One of the ultimate goals of any organisation should be to give customers the best possible service. In turn, those customers will recommend you and use your services again.

Consistent performance. Consistency is vital in any organisation. Staff should be performing at the same high level every day. Strong training and development increases consistency in performance. This is especially true when companies are continuously evolving in the pursuit of improvement.

Stronger motivation. Most of us want to improve and be the best that we can be. Call it achievement, self-actualisation or whatever you want, but reaching our full potential gives us more motivation to do our job. We want to feel part of the organisation and we want to feel valued. No one wants to feel as though they're just another number going through the motions. So, it's important to tailor individual training and development plans to the needs of the learner as well as the needs of the business. I've seen too many training plans that are too generic, benefiting half the learners while the other half are ignored.

Increased productivity. If staff have the knowledge to do their job better, more efficiently and to a higher standard, it stands to reason that productivity will increase. How can it not? The secret to an effective training plan – and, therefore, increased productivity over a sustained period – is that training and learning should be constant. Companies tend to train staff on a set of procedures and leave it at that. They think their responsibility has ended there. That's so far removed from what should be happening. Continuous improvement is exactly that – continuous.

Increased profit. In conversations with many companies, the argument I come up against time and again is that it costs money, time and effort to put in place a company training and development plan. These business owners aren't able to see the bigger picture – they're blinkered by the lack of systemisation in their business. It's a chicken-and-egg situation: as soon as the business is systemised they'll see the value of training and development, but they haven't got time to get the business to that point. Yes, you will have to invest in the short term, but the rewards in the medium to long term far outweigh the initial outlay.

Reduced cost and wastage. When employees don't perform to their potential, it's usually down to lack of training, especially if poor performance continues over a period of time. Every time a member of staff does something wrong, it needs to be corrected. The employee has to do the task again, someone else has to do it or, even worse, you have to do it. This costs the company money and is a waste of time.

Seven steps to developing an effective individual training and development plan

When running a business, it's so important to ensure that you have the right people in the right roles and that everyone is fully trained. Many companies put training and development low down on the priority list, so they're never going to come up with a specific training and development plan. What's even more frustrating is that it isn't complicated to do.

This section is vital to the ongoing training and development of your staff – and, therefore, the overall success of systemising your business. The two go hand in hand.

Training and development, like the systemisation of the business, is an evolving process. You can't simply write a manual, train employees once and forget about it. You need to review, improve and tweak your plan when needed.

Step 1 – Identify goals. To come up with an effective training and development plan, you need to identify the initial goals. This is easier than you might think. Ask yourself the following questions.

- What do I want learners to achieve?
- What's my vision for the training?

- Do my employees need to learn some things before others?
- How will learners know when they have achieved the individual goals?
- What are the company's needs?

These goals will dictate how you approach the training plan. You need to agree them before the training starts.

The goals are vital to the success of the training plan – it's that simple.

Step 2 – Create training materials. This is an extremely important part of the process. As mentioned earlier, simply handing the staff the procedures to learn or reading them out won't give you the best results, although alongside other learning materials this has its place. You will have to put some effort and time into this. Remember to include several types of learning materials to cater to the different learning styles. Here are some tips:

- Visual learners – use slides or video.
- Auditory learners – use audios and podcasts.
- Kinaesthetic learners – include games, demonstrate procedures and let the learners try for themselves.
- Group work can bring out the best in people. It helps them to see other perspectives. Be mindful, though, that some people do not perform well in groups. You will need to make sure that they are not overwhelmed by more extrovert characters in the group.

- Take into account the differences in the left and right sides of the brain. Some people are more logical and others are more creative. This affects which type of training they get the most out of.
- Use humour and games and have as much fun as possible. Learners will react better, pay more attention and retain information far more easily if they are having fun than if they feel under pressure or bored.

LEFT SIDE   RIGHT SIDE

Spoken and Written Language

Sequencing

Word Analysis

Filling Forms

Numbers

Letters

Analytical

Logical

Abstract

Thinks in the Past and Future

Nonverbal Information
Music   Images

Drawing

Construction

Voice Tones

Creative

Intuitive

Spatial Relationships
Faces   Shapes   Maps

Concrete

Thinks in the Present

Step 3 – Create a training schedule. Depending on the length of the procedures and what your training goals are, it could take anything from a few weeks to a few months to roll out your procedural training. Bear in mind the following when creating your schedule.

- Don't rush the training. It takes as long as it takes – we all learn at different speeds.
- Don't put too much pressure on new members of staff. If after their probation they have not retained or utilised the information provided through training, you'll need to make a business decision about whether to continue their employment.
- Stick to the training plan. If you miss a session due to workload or some other reason, it sets a precedent for your staff.
- Keep the skills training matrix updated (see Chapter 2).
- Don't expect learners to understand everything the first time. Plan for additional time so your staff can fully understand a procedure before moving on to the next one. If your training material is competent and the matrix is continually completed, you will always know where the learners are in relation to their training and development plan.

Step 4 – Decide who will do the training. Initially it might be you, the business owner, who carries out the training. I accept that doing all the work yourself seems to go against the grain of this book and the theory of systemisation. In the early days, though, you may have to be all things to all people, depending on your financial resources and time.

If you're carrying out the training, you can't be involved as the person who wrote the systems – you need to put your training hat on. When system designers or authors become heavily involved in the training process, it can lead to undesirable results. It's important not to take things to heart if people don't understand the processes. Be open to criticism and suggestions for improvement, which are part of the feedback loop.

If training isn't your thing, consider hiring someone to do that job or temporarily delegating the responsibility to another staff member. I initially trained all my employees myself, but then I hired a consultant, who did a much better job. Eventually I promoted an existing member of staff to help with training and development. This was partly a financial decision but it was also a control issue. Having our own training department meant we could roll out training as and when it was needed. This made a huge difference to our staff and the speed at which they learn.

Step 5 – Set expectations. Before any training meeting, tell people what the training is about. This sets expectations and the standard you must work to. If you take training and development seriously you can expect your staff to, too. Continual communication helps with the way in which it is received.

This is also a great time to answer any questions that employees attending the training may have. Sometimes, people think they don't need to attend a particular course or refresher. This may be a good time to show them exactly why you think it is relevant to them. Perhaps they haven't performed in line with company objectives so additional training is required. Rather than having an embarrassing conversation in front of the other learners, you can address these concerns beforehand and make sure everyone is perfectly aligned with the training and development objectives.

Step 6 - Track progress. If you use the learning objectives for each procedure and you keep updating the training matrix, it will be straightforward to track individual progress towards company aims. You could also carry out regular one-to-ones to discuss employees' progress and find out what you can do to make their learning experience better.

The ultimate goal of systems training is for staff to be able to follow the procedures and perform to company standards. If they're not performing, it's down to one of two things:

1. **Lack of skill.** This is a training issue. With a well-thought-out and balanced training programme, this will happen less and less.

2. **Lack of will.** This is a motivation issue. The person has chosen not to follow the procedures. In my experience, this can be down to laziness or cutting corners. A robust training plan that ties in with an audit process will help prevent these issues. (More on this in the Audit section.).

Step 7 – Welcome feedback. With any training programme, you need effective feedback to see where you're doing well and where things could be improved. In my experience, many people don't appreciate constructive feedback and even shy away from it. Maybe it's a British thing, but people often get offended when others suggest improvements. But, as Bill Gates said: "We all need people who give us feedback. That's how we improve."

I once had an excellent business mentor who used to sit in on our managers' meetings. After every meeting, he would spend ten minutes with me explaining what I'd done well and what I needed to improve on. I really looked forward to these sessions, because this was the type of feedback I wouldn't get from my managers, who would be polite, clap at the right moments and laugh on cue at my terrible jokes. Flattering as it was, it wasn't going to help me grow as a businessman.

My mentor once picked me up on the fact that I swore in a managers' meeting – a major faux pas, and I didn't even notice I'd done it. It was hard to listen to this feedback, but it was important and I made sure it didn't happen again.

Feedback from learners – on individual sessions and group activities – is vital to improving the quality of the session. If the overall trust isn't there, the feedback will not be as forthcoming. This means you need to create a culture of welcoming feedback, which is easier said than done.

You can do this by not overreacting or taking feedback personally. The first time you overreact to feedback you think is unfair, your staff will stop providing it. If you're the best trainer in the world and your learners are wrong, that isn't a problem – but we all know that isn't true.

If your employees are apprehensive about giving feedback, an anonymous survey could help. Feedback collected in this way will be less accurate and revealing than feedback given in a culture of openness and transparency, but it's still better than no feedback at all.

You don't have to ask people lots of questions. I've seen feedback forms with as few as two questions: "What did you like about the training session?" and "What didn't you like about the training session?" An example training evaluation form is shown below.

Training Evaluation Form

		Strongly Agree	Agree	Neutral	Disagree	Strongly Disagree
1.	The training met my expectations	○	○	○	○	○
2.	I will be able to apply the knowledge learned	○	○	○	○	○
3.	The training objectives for each topic were identified and followed	○	○	○	○	○
4.	The content was organised and easy to follow	○	○	○	○	○
5.	The materials distributed were useful	○	○	○	○	○
6.	The trainer was knowledgeable	○	○	○	○	○
7.	The quality of instruction as good	○	○	○	○	○
8.	The trainer met the training objectives	○	○	○	○	○
9.	Class participation and interaction were encouraged	○	○	○	○	○
10.	Adequate time was provided for questions and discussion	○	○	○	○	○

		Excellent	Good	Average	Poor	Very poor
11.	How do you rate the training overall	○	○	○	○	○

12 . What aspects of the training could be improved?

13. Other comments

THANK YOU FOR YOUR PARTICIPATION!

Once you've collated all the feedback, you need another dose of brutal honesty. Is the feedback relevant to the training? In other words, do your learners have a point? Be humble in the pursuit of continuous improvement – if they do have a point and you need to adapt or evolve your training, do it without stomping around like a bear with a sore head or taking it out on your staff. Make sure you thank people for their feedback and tell them you have improved the training.

This will have a huge impact on learners and improve your sessions. Everyone wins.

Training paperwork

Documenting training isn't the most exciting part of the training cycle, but it is one of the most important. Why do you document your business plan, your finances, your procedures and your client contracts? Documenting training is just as important for the following reasons:

1. It helps you to keep track of what training has been planned and received so you can review it regularly and be held accountable.
2. It ensures there is no ambiguity about what training has been agreed.
3. If you win the lottery tomorrow or get hit by a bus, someone else can take over.

4. If formal action is required as part of staff performance management, the training documents will be invaluable to your case.

So, what should you document? Used alone, the following processes will benefit your businesses training investment. Use both of them and you have a really effective process that you can roll out to train almost any team.

- Skills training matrix
- Individual learning plan.

Skills training matrix

A skills training matrix is a simple way of defining what skills are required for each role. And where people are in relation to needing the skills to be successful in that role. It allows managers and team members to appraise how effectively they have demonstrated a skill over a set period. This may be a probation period or another agreed timeframe. It's a great tool to use with new starters and allows you to have a conversation about individuals' perceived effectiveness against what is needed in the role.

A job description is a great place to start, as this is the measure of what you want a person to bring to your business when you recruit them. You can always refer back to it at a later stage, too.

I tried a few different rating systems before I found what works for us. I have included this simple system below. There are other good systems out there, so keeping trying them until you find the one that's most appropriate for you and your business.

I would encourage you not to include a rating for "average". Forcing an appraisal to sit on one side or the other of average ensures that managers make decisions and don't just take the easy route.

If you give managers the opportunity to rate an employee from one to five, most will choose the rating of three because they don't want to hurt the person's feelings by selecting a lower rating. The middle of the road doesn't attract attention. Anything less attracts negative attention: people want to understand why someone isn't performing better. That's fine if you want a business where average performance slips under the radar. People might not be entirely comfortable with being forced to get off the fence, but this is the only way to know whether employees are performing well or whether they need more training or support.

The four performance criteria we use are:

1. **Underperforming.** The team member might not have had to use the skill being measured before. They may have demonstrated the skill at a higher level in the past but shown a decline due to a change in a process, a system or their mind-set.
2. **Developing.** The team member is developing the measured skill with coaching, training and practice, but they have not achieved the expected results yet.

3. **Performing.** The team member is displaying the skill consistently and achieving the expected results, but there is room to develop further.

4. **Exceeding.** The team member is displaying the skill at an exceptional level for their role and is able to coach and mentor others to develop their skills.

To record your skills matrix and appraisals, you can use anything from a printed form to a sophisticated software tool. I use the simple Excel spreadsheet below. This makes it easy to keep developing your skills-appraisal approach.

Skills Matrix - Portfolio Manager			
Name: John Smith		Branch: Hartlepool	
Ref	Behaviours	Score	Performance Level
1	Positive attitude	3	Performing
2	Solution and results focused	3	Performing
3	Results orientated	2	Developing
4	Professionalism	4	Exceeding
5	Flexible approach	3	Performing
6	Committed to personal development	2	Developing
	Key competencies	**3**	
7	Ability to deliver excellent customer service as per charter	3	Performing
8	Developed time-management skills to ensure effective management of own resources	2	Developing
9	Ability to work under own initiative and as part of a team	3	Performing
10	Determination to secure new business with focused action	4	Exceeding
11	Negotiation skills to achieve the best outcome for the business and the customer	4	Exceeding
12	Conflict resolution within own levels of authority	3	Performing
13	Effectivley manage staff	3	Performing
14	Enhanced communication skills	2	Developing
	Key activities (linked to KPIs)		
15	Chases arrears	3	Performing

Behaviours. This refers to specific aspects of how you want your staff member to behave. You can rate each aspect of their behaviour accordingly. Always make sure you can back up the score with evidence and examples.

For example, at Castledene, once we have evidenced that a member of staff has a positive attitude in all situations and they have been scored a four, we expect them to keep up that attitude at all times. Now, we are not robots and we don't expect people to have a smile on their face 24/7. We need to be pragmatic and warm in our approach to our staff. Having said that, if someone scores a four, they shouldn't consistently go down to a three. You can't undo the knowledge they have evidenced to hit a four. As difficult as it may be, the company must come first. If people are not showing the values or behaviours you expect, you should manage them out of the business.

Key competencies. Key competencies are the skills that you expect an employee to have to be able to do their job. Most people won't have all these skills from day one. As you train and develop them, their skills will grow and improve.

Again, a person shouldn't go backwards in their skill ratings. If they start to underperform, use the skills matrix to relate their performance back to their previous higher score. As brutal as this sounds, this evidence helps you if you need to performance-manage someone out the business. Progression, not perfection, is the key. You can't expect people to be perfect from day one, but you can expect them to improve at an acceptable rate.

Key activities linked to KPIs. Linking tasks in people's job descriptions to certain KPIs means that you can measure their performance. The main advantage of KPIs is that people either achieve them or they don't, giving you factual evidence to help you manage people. As most KPIs are linked to the profitability of the company, you can also see the effect that individual employees have on the business at all times.

If someone is achieving most of their KPIs, they may feel that they are a valuable asset to the company. While that may be true, if they're not hitting all their KPIs after receiving training, this suggests that they might not be the ideal person for the job. You only want the best staff for your business, whether they're the best from day one or you work to help them become the best. As a company, you only want to keep people who want to better themselves.

	Key activities (linked to KPIs)		
15	Chases arrears	3	Performing
16	Follow up viewings and feedback to landlords	2	Developing
17	Process appointments and feedback to landlord	1	Underperforming
18	Ensure that property maintenance issues are resolved in a timely & cost effective manner (including CP12's etc)	2	Developing
19	Ensure MLIT's are up to date for vacant properties	3	Performing
20	Answer all incoming communications (internal and external)	3	Performing
21	Deal with customer enquiries effectively (see customer service charter)	4	Exceeding
22	Ensure focus on own development	4	Exceeding
23	Resolve complaints	3	Performing
24	Escalate queries outside of own authority level	2	Developing
25	Maintain compliance with industry and internal regulations	3	Performing
26	Attention to all H&S issues, including hazard and accident reporting	2	Developing

Individual learning plan

An individual learning plan (ILP) helps you track employees' progress towards agreed goals and improvement activities. It should be updated after each review or development activity.

A key purpose of an ILP is to give each member of staff responsibility for their learning and for updating their ILP. Some managers shy away from this, usually because of the same old barrier to effective delegation – the belief that "they won't do it as well as I do". As a business leader or owner, you need to delegate to achieve the purpose of the systemisation process. Documenting your own ILP is manageable. Grow your business and find yourself documenting fifty or one hundred ILPs and it will take over your life. We need to empower staff, especially managers, to complete their own ILPs.

Use the documenting process as a coaching opportunity. Tell your staff what to include in their ILP and what level of detail you expect. The main reason for passing ownership to your teams is to give them a sense of control. If they feel responsible for their own development, they will feel in control of it.

There are four steps to creating and documenting an ILP. You can use these as table headings as a simple way of documenting and reviewing an ILP.

1. **Identify development needs.** Have an honest and open skills appraisal with the employee. Together, decide where they are at now and where they need to get to if they're to

become a valuable member of your team based on your company's skills matrix. Once the person has been working with you for a short while, you will instinctively know what needs to be developed.

2. **Consider development activities.** Think about how you can help the employee to develop in the areas you have identified together. Will you do that yourself or get someone in who has more experience? You might have to train someone else to do this so you can take a step back. Identifying a leader in your business helps with this.

3. **Set SMART goals for development activities.** Pay particular attention to the time-bound aspect, as this is likely to have a direct impact on how efficiently the results are delivered.

4. **Review and evaluate the ILP.** I cannot stress this enough. If you don't evaluate the outcome of the development activity from the last session, training is a waste of time and energy. Use your skills matrix to record improvements in skills, or use direct observations and feedback to build your team's confidence that they are heading in the right direction. Knowing how and in which areas your employees are developing is vitally important to your business.

Don't overcomplicate training and development. Start small and work your way up, adding to your training and development programmes and ILPs over a number of years. The main thing is to make sure that they work for you and your staff.

RECAP

In this chapter, you've learned the following:

- People are motivated by progressing, and training and development is the best way to instil that motivation.
- People have varying learning styles.
- A mix of learning material is essential for the best results.
- Individual training and development leads to:
  - Less time spent on management
  - Addressing employees' weaknesses
  - Consistent performance
  - Stronger motivation
  - Increased productivity
  - Increased profit
  - Reduced cost and waste.
- The seven steps to an effective individual training and development plan are:
  1. Identify goals
  2. Create training materials
  3. Create a training schedule
  4. Identify who is doing the training
  5. Set expectations
  6. Track progress
  7. Welcome feedback.

Task

- Using the example skills training matrix, come up with your own individual learning and training plan for you or your staff. Include behaviours and competencies and link performance to your KPIs.

- Trial it, test it and tweak it. Make sure you cover off as much information/actions in the skills training matrix and ILP.

THREE

AUDITING

Make Sure You're
Following The Rules

This, for me, is the most underused and underrated part of the five-part systemisation framework. Auditing is essential to ensuring that systemisation works. Without it, no matter how good your operations manual or how great your training and development, you'll start to move backwards and mistakes will happen and go unchecked.

An audit gives you confidence that your procedures are working and your employees are performing as the business requires.

In our daily lives, we audit pretty much everything – it's second nature. Every time we have the car washed, we inspect it to make sure nothing has been missed. When the online food shopping arrives, we check the items off against the order list. Every time we go shopping for clothes we see whether they fit and whether they have any defects. We were all audited at school by the exam at the end of term. We audit and are audited in every part of our personal lives, so why should auditing in business be any different?

In my experience, few businesses audit. This is shocking. How do we know if our employees are making mistakes? Not everyone will complain when they receive poor service; not everyone brings it to the attention of the manager. You can only imagine the number of times I've heard people say after a negative event, "If only I'd known so-and-so was doing this" or "If only I'd known so-and-so hadn't done that". If they had audited their business, they would have had a good chance of picking up on the mistake sooner. Will an audit pick up every mistake a member of staff ever makes? Of course not. What it does is change the culture of the business from an attitude of "That'll do" to one of "I'm going to do this the best I can".

Landlords we work with sometimes tell us that they decided to change letting agents because the previous agent gave them poor service. When we take over a property from another agent, we ask for the property file. This should contain various pieces of information, some required by law and others that are simply best industry practice. I'm yet to see a file that I'm truly impressed with. Unfortunately, in many cases we have to break the news to the landlord that they weren't legally covered for certain things. I don't believe for one second that the previous agent didn't know they had to meet certain legal requirements. I believe they didn't have the right processes in place and they didn't audit to ensure their services and procedures were consistent.

When we lose properties (yes, we do lose properties), we want the agent taking over to be amazed by how good the files are. Sounds a bit cheesy? Not in the slightest – we take pride in our work and we want other agents to be impressed. This consistency is only possible with regular and intense audits, ensuring the same high quality of paperwork every time.

It's human nature to slack off when we know we're not being watched. I do this myself. If I go to the gym on my own, I don't always lift the heaviest weights I can and I might not do as many sets – and this is coming from someone who played sport professionally and loves the gym. A good procedural audit in a business shouts out, "If you slack off, you'll be found out". It takes time and effort to get complete buy-in from staff, but once you've done that people even start looking forward to the auditing process. For example, in my business the audit plays a big part in which branch is chosen as branch of the month. This motivates employees to put forward their files to the area manager rather than hiding them away and hoping they won't be picked. It's great to see that your employees are proud of their work and want to be noticed for it.

Employees may see auditing as Big Brother watching them, and some members of staff will think you're doing it to check up on them. Let's be honest: you are. Remember, you want the business to be the best it can be and you want to give your employees the chance to be the best versions of themselves, so why not give them the best tools? Auditing is a way of helping people improve. By identifying their weaknesses, you can provide training and development in certain areas so they can do better.

I got buy-in from staff by explaining that we wanted to be the best and we were not apologising for that. They understood this. I then explained that to be the best, we need to understand where we are weakest: by doing so, we can improve our processes and procedures to ensure that they, and the company, become the best in the UK. I also said that although we would highlight some basic issues with their work and the procedures, with time and training we would all improve and grow together.

Why audit?

You need to audit for the following reasons.

To achieve management priorities. Businesses move quickly and priorities change. Auditing the business can align management priorities with operational priorities.

For example, a few years ago we changed how we managed some of our branches, placing much more emphasis on data and KPIs. Operationally it wasn't a huge task, but the change in mind-set that managers had to make certainly was. We became, and still are, a results-based company. We began setting targets for managers, and KPIs formed a big part of that. This works well for audits, as it takes the emotion out of the process and focuses on the facts: either you achieve your targets or you don't.

To meet the requirements of management systems, regulations, contracts and the law. This is especially relevant in the property industry, where there are frequent regulatory and legislative changes. It can be worrying to work in an industry where the threat of legal action is all too common. An audit checks whether you have adapted your procedures to comply with any changes and whether your employees are keeping to those changes.

I'll let you into a secret. Since I started the business in 2008, apart from in the first six months there hasn't been a single day when we haven't been dealing with a legal case or a case with the Property Ombudsman against us. Its just the nature of the industry. Thanks to our procedures and audits we've never lost a case, which shows that the audit trail works.

When you work in a litigious industry, audits are a necessary part of dealing with that. They help make your company bulletproof.

To meet the requirements for evaluating suppliers. If you use any suppliers in any shape or form, you need to know if they are performing to your standards. Their work may affect your reputation and brand, so it's essential that you only work with people who you trust and who share your vision and values. This is easier said than done. Contractors often start off well but get complacent and perform less well over time.

Auditing can keep contractors and suppliers on their toes and make them think twice about cutting corners. It won't catch every problem, but it will pick up on most. This could be seen as trying to catch suppliers out, but if you blindly trust that everything is going to be fine and you don't audit them, you're asking for trouble.

To meet customer requirements. Different customers will have different needs. In my opinion, great customer service is about finding out what your customers' needs and motivations are and meeting them on an individual basis. Of course, you can't bend over backwards for every customer, but you can tailor your service to suit them.

Taking my own business as an example, while most landlords we work with want us to pay their portion of the rent as soon as we receive it from tenants, a few want us to hold on to the rent until the start of the month. We audit the business to check that we have tailored our services and we have met customers' needs.

To assess risks to the organisation. An audit not only aligns well with legislative requirements but also takes into account other risks to the business, such as theft and fraud.

For example, an employee stole from the company. How did we find out, even though they worked a hundred miles away from? It was all down to KPIs and audits. The KPIs highlighted an anomaly in the financial takings. We immediately carried out an impromptu audit and discovered some money had been taken. All this happened in three days. Just imagine if we hadn't had the KPIs and auditing process in place – how long could the employee have done this for and how many customers would have had their money stolen? My company would have suffered terrible damage to its reputation. Thanks to the audit, every penny was recovered and no one lost out.

Audit objectives

The internal audit is a systematic and documented process to verify, independently and objectively, whether an organisation's quality-management system conforms to the processes and procedures set out in the operations manual.

In plain English, that means it tells you whether or not you're following your operations manual.

As an auditor, you are not concerned with people's feelings or excuses. Your only focus is to ensure that you audit against the operations manual. This may seem robotic and unfeeling, but if you want your business to improve or to be the best in your area or industry, you need to take this approach.

Audit paperwork

The two biggest issues that people have when it comes to auditing are how to carry out an audit and what paperwork is needed. The good news is that it's not as complicated as you might think.

You need four main audit documents:

- Internal audit schedule
- Audit checklist
- Corrective action report
- Deviations and corrective action log.

If you want to go all out on auditing your business, you can use standards, such as ISO 9001:2000, as your benchmark. ISO is a great way to audit your business but it's paperwork-heavy, so use what works for your company and leave what doesn't. Remember, having something is better than having nothing.

Internal Audit Schedule

How often you audit specific procedures will be dependant on the importance and complexity of the procedures. Please ensure that all procedures are audited as per agreed schedule and be as diligent as possible. All feedback is to be given to senior management within 3 days of audit unless MNC suggest sooner.

Section No.	Title	Dept/ Section	Audit Frequency	
			Monthly	Annually
1	Marketing of property	Lettings		
2	Valuations	Lettings		
3	Carrying out an inspeection	Lettings		
4	Eviction proceedings	Lettings		
5	Compliance paperwork	Lettings		
6	Dealing with complaints	Lettings		
7	Prospecting	Lettings		
8	Paying rent to landlord	Accounts		
9	Chasing arrears	Accounts		
10	Paying contractors	Accounts		

Internal audit schedule

This is like a diary for the auditing process. It highlights what you need to audit and when. Many templates are available, but I've found that the one below (works best. You can also download the template from my website at www.the5partsystem.com

This audit schedule reflects the ISO 9001:2008 standard. Decide which sections are most important to your business – in other words, which processes will affect your customers most if there are any problems. These are the processes that you must make sure are stable and consistent. You might wish to schedule these processes for extra audits – perhaps two or three times a year. Develop the example schedule further to make it relevant to your company.

									Form: 25		
									Version: 1		

					Planned Audit						
Jan	**Feb**	**Mar**	**Apr**	**May**	**Jun**	**Jul**	**Aug**	**Sept**	**Oct**	**Nov**	**Dec**
✓						✓					
		✓			✓			✓			✓
✓								✓			
				✓						✓	
✓	✓	✓	✓	✓	✓	✓	✓	✓	✓	✓	✓
	✓					✓					
		✓			✓			✓			✓
			✓				✓				✓
		✓				✓				✓	
				✓						✓	

Version. Always make sure you can easily identify the version number so you can check you are using the latest version. Once you start using more forms you'll see how easily mistakes can happen. There may be only a small difference between the latest version and the previous one, but that small change could be important.

Title. It's important to identify which procedure you are auditing against. The person or department being audited may want to focus more on that procedure before the audit, especially if they have a few months' notice. This tells employees which aspects of the business are most important.

Audit Frequency. Record how often you need to audit a particular procedure. Audit procedures that are critical to the organisation more often than those that are less critical. Procedures that have legal or regulatory consequences will need to be audited at least once a month. For example, we audit our property files once a month to check that we are complying with the various regulations on letting a property. As 80% of our complaints relate to tenant selection, we place importance on auditing our tenant-selection and application processes. Auditing often tells employees that this procedure is not to be compromised. For procedures where there are fewer issues, carry out audits less frequently; for example, we audit the viewing process once a quarter. If the viewing process does go wrong, we can pick it up at the tenant application stage, so this procedure has a safety net.

Planned Audit. This is where you can schedule the dates for the audits listed. This gives your staff plenty of time to prepare for the audit and do what it takes to get their branch or department running like clockwork. There is a school of thought that says that unscheduled (surprise) audits are just as useful, as staff should always be prepared for an audit. I'm not a huge fan of this idea, as I think it's important to work with your staff by encouraging improvements rather than trying to catch them out by springing an audit on them unannounced.

Audit checklist

Complete this document while you are carrying out the audit. Again, it can be a simple document – there's no point in overcomplicating it. I like to keep things as simple and smooth as possible.

Audit Title. This might seem an obvious thing to include, but a company I worked for previously used an audit checklist with no procedure titles or references. Although I eventually worked out which procedure I was auditing from the questions in the checklist, I wasted valuable time in doing so.

Audit Questions. This is an essential part of the audit checklist. Writing the questions can be time-consuming but they make things so much more efficient. To come up with the questions, read your procedures and decide which processes you want to audit. Then ask the most detailed questions possible, using SMART objectives. Think about even the smallest details, such as

"Was the form signed by the branch manager?" and "Was the process completed in the agreed 24 hours?" Every little detail is fair game here – nothing is off-limits. The more questions you ask, the more in-depth your audit will be.

The smallest number of questions we have for auditing a procedure is ten and the largest is thirty-five. There is no optimum number of questions: this will vary from business to business and industry to industry and will reflect how detailed your procedures are. Ours are pretty detailed, so we like to ask a lot of questions. We don't want anything, especially regulations, to come back and bite us later on. Here is an example audit checklist.

Audit Checklist

PROCEDURE – 7.0 TENANT APPLICATION PROCESS

Q No	Audit Questions	Findings (tick)	
		Compliant	OFI
1	Has all information on Form 5 been completed?		
2	Have we received email acceptance from the Landlord?		
3	Has the tenant paid a deposit?		
4	Is the deposit registered (reference no)?		
5	Has the tenant a guarantor?		
6	Have they completed Document 8 & 10?		
7	Has the inventory been carried out as per Procedure 14?		
8	Has the tenant signed it		
9	Has the inventory been sent to the Landlord?		
10	Have we received and acted on feedback from Landlord?		
Auditor's Name		Initials	

Findings. There are four categories in the findings section. If the audit question is answered "yes" and there are no issues, it is compliant and you tick the relevant box. Tick this box only if the procedure has been implemented and followed correctly.

If an opportunity for improvement has been highlighted by either you or the person or department being audited, tick the opportunity for improvement (OFI) box.

			Form:36	
			Version: 3	
		Audit Evidence	Opportunities for Improvement	
Minor NC	Major NC	Provide references to documentations or records that justify the finding	Provide suggestions for process improvement	
		Date		

A minor non-conformance is when the question is partly answered "yes", but there is incomplete evidence to show that the procedure has been followed. Minor non-conformance will not result in the failure of the process and there are no regulatory or legal repercussions. You will probably just feel frustrated with the person you are auditing and want to say, "What a silly mistake, you should have known better".

A major non-conformance is exactly what it sounds like. It means there has been a clear omission of documentary evidence and the questions have not been answered "yes". This may leave the company open to further action being taken against it, such as legal action. It may point to poor customer service or a product being delivered that could damage the reputation of your name, brand or company.

Audit Evidence. As with everything to do with audits, make sure you include as much evidence as possible. When you give the feedback to the department heads, especially if it isn't good news, they will ask you to prove your findings. So, rather than have those difficult conversations, it's best to pre-empt them by detailing all the evidence beforehand. For example, you could photocopy all the major and minor non-conformances and highlight them in your report.

When I started doing audits and I found non-conformances, I didn't write them down. When I gave the feedback to the branch manager at the time, she said "I don't believe you". I was a bit taken aback, but I didn't have anything to back up my claim that she and her branch hadn't performed in the way I had expected. A few hours later, I brought the evidence to her and the feedback session was far more productive. Evidence is key to a good audit and will make feedback sessions go much more smoothly.

Opportunities for Improvement. I've also heard this called preventive measures. In essence, they are the same. Preventive measures are pro-active – they are actions to stop something happening or stop it getting too serious. If something has already gone wrong, it is called a non-conformance and you deal with it by taking corrective action. Opportunities for improvement are when you see something that has the potential to go wrong but it hasn't gone wrong yet. For example, when you notice a loophole in the process or the potential for something to go wrong or fail. The audit is the perfect time to mention this.

Corrective action report

A corrective action report (CAR) is a way of recording anything that has gone wrong, be it a minor or major non-conformance. Don't get too worked up about the language. A non-conformance is an issue that has arisen from the audit when procedures haven't been followed correctly.

Here is an example CAR form.

Corrective Action Report (CAR)		
Date:	**Auditor:**	**Form No: 21**
CAR No:	**Dept:**	**Rev: 03**
Description of non-conformity		
Root Cause		
Action taken to prevent reoccurrence		
Action by:		Target date:
Review of action		
Reviewed by:		Review date:

CAR Number. All corrective action reports need to be recorded for monitoring purposes. You can use them to identify trends in the company and you can look at individual corrective action reports to analyse these trends in further detail.

Description of non-conformance. Include as much detail as possible here. Refer to the exact procedure and clause. Include all the evidence needed to prove the non-conformance. Make sure you include copies of all relevant paperwork, photos and so on.

Root cause. Write a statement about what caused the non-conformance. Remember to use facts and evidence, not heresy. The statement may be needed as part of an employee's performance management, so everything needs to be factual.

Action taken to prevent reoccurrence. This could be additional training (most likely) or an improvement to the process or procedure. Be impartial here and give an open and honest assessment of what is needed to avoid the situation happening again.

Review of effectiveness of action taken. Always follow up an non-conformance report. The exact time you do this will depend on what the non-conformance was and what action needed to prevent it happening again.

Dates. Dates are always important in auditing to ensure continual improvement. Make sure someone has to follow up the corrective action reports on a certain date to check that the corrective action has been completed. If it has and a satisfactory outcome has been achieved, you can close the non-conformance report. If the action has not been completed, you must set a new review date and make sure the action is complete by that date.

Signatures. Again, this may seem like a small detail, but it's so important to take ownership in business, be that ownership of a success, an issue or an action. We need to be held accountable if we are to improve.

You might be wondering what the point of going to all this trouble is. If you know what went wrong, can't you just put it right straight away and forget about it?

Firstly, the bigger you get as a business and the more staff you employ, the harder this becomes. Other things get in the way and priorities change. You might forget what action is needed to put a non-conformance right or forget to review it.

You also need to record information so you can hold individuals accountable in all aspects of business, especially when things don't go the way they should. If not, you might not realise that a particular person is always making mistakes or a certain process never works properly. By keeping a clear record using corrective action reports forms, you can see any trends and deal with them accordingly.

Log your corrective action reports on a register. This keeps all corrective action reports in one place and makes it much easier to spot trends. The larger the organisation, especially if there is more than one internal auditor, the harder it is to see when certain types of issues are happening regularly.

An example register is shown below.

Corrective Action Report Log

List all the corrective actions, complaints, and their related casues(s), corrective action(s), preventative measures, if any procedures have been modified. Record that staff have been trained and developed on the new procedures

Date / Time of CAR / Complaint	CAR / Complaint Description	Corrective Action	Prevention of Reoccurence (Eg - Training or Process)	New Procedure	Employees Trained on Procedure	Signature of Person Responsible

Date/Time of CAR or Complaint. This is a small but important detail, as it will tell you whether issues are occurring regularly or if they are one-offs.

CAR/Complaint Description. Always put in as much detail as you can. If the auditor leaves the organisation, whoever takes over needs to be able to quickly understand the issues.

Corrective Action. What did you do to ensure the non-conformance won't happen again? Detailing it here will give you a greater understanding of what works and what doesn't.

Prevention of Reoccurrence. When things go wrong in a company it's down to a person, a process or equipment.

New Procedure. If it was a procedure, have you changed it so the problem doesn't happen again?

Employees Trained on Procedure. Have your employees had training to ensure that the issue won't happen again? For example, if you changed the procedure, have staff been trained on it?

Signature of Person Responsible. This tells you who is accountable for training staff, updating processes and putting in place the corrective actions. The whole point of auditing is to make people accountable for their actions, even at the level of signing off procedures and at senior management level. No one is above being held accountable.

How to carry out an audit

Now we know what documents are involved in an audit, we need to understand how to carry out an audit.

According to ISO 9000, which is the international benchmark standard for auditing, an audit is "a systematic, independent and documented process, for obtaining audit evidence and evaluating it objectively to determine to which extent the audit criteria are fulfilled". In layman's terms, it checks that we're following the procedures and doing what we're meant to be doing.

Audits should be planned, objective, and carried out in a formal way. You may have to audit procedures that involve your friends, and you need to highlight any shortfalls or non-conformities if you are to improve your business. If people are making mistakes or not following procedures, you need to report it.

It goes without saying that when you're trusting someone to bring any issues in the business to the attention of the business owner or senior management team, that person needs to be competent at the auditing process. Remember, the auditing process is more important that the process you are auditing. This is why external auditors can be a great help, even though they don't work in your business. In fact, sometimes this is an advantage. External auditors come in and follow the procedures to the letter. If they work, great; if not, they complete an NCR. If an auditor is from the industry, they may overlook certain issues because they automatically understand and forgive minor failings in a process.

Plan your audit

To get the best from your audit, you need to plan it thoroughly. You need to do two things:

1. **Create and use an audit schedule.** This will tell you when and what department or process you are auditing.
2. **Read and understand the process you will be auditing.** This will help you to ask probing questions and reduce the chances of someone trying to pull the wool over your eyes.

As with most things, careful planning leads to a much smoother operation. Your audit will be more efficient and more effective if you spend more time preparing for it.

Audit effectively

To be as effective as possible when auditing, you need to do four main things. Anything less and you are not doing your auditing process as much justice as you should.

1. **Interview employees.** Based on your audit planning and checklist questions, ask people about their work. Listen to what they tell you and see if their explanations match the written procedures. This will give you a good indication of whether people understand what they are supposed to be

doing, which will form part of your recommendations. Use open-ended and probing questions (not just questions that only need a "yes" or "no" answer) to get as much useful information as you can. Don't be afraid to challenge, to probe and to follow an audit trail to see where it leads you.

2. **Observe operations.** I've always been a people-watcher. If you sit back and watch what people do and how they do it, inevitably you'll understand why they do what they do. Aid your own understanding of the process by watching it being performed. Of course, you don't have to do this every time, especially if your business is small. But if you're auditing parts of your business that someone else has set up and runs, this will help you. This type of audit is also less disruptive, as it allows people to get on with their work while you audit.

3. **Review documents and records.** Ask the people you're auditing what documents and records they use in their work and relate this back to the procedures manual. If most of your processes have forms that need to be completed and appendixes that need to be attached, checking whether this has been done is an easy way to audit the process. Verify that the records described in the documents are being collected and controlled correctly. In other words, are people using the latest version? This sounds obvious, but it's easy to fall foul of it. For example, one of our employees signed a client up using an old

management agreement, which we had changed in line with new legislation.

It's also important to challenge the need for documentation and try to find more effective ways of managing and controlling the processes you're auditing. An audit should help the company to adapt and grow – it's not a one-page document that has no value and won't be used.

4. **Examine records.** Auditors cannot interview every employee, observe every activity, check every document and evaluate every record. You should strive to use representative samples that allow you to make informed judgements. We move in sixty to seventy tenants a month, so we take a sample of 20% from that month. Employees don't know which files will be taken, so they do their best in case their file is the one that's audited. Since audits are limited due to sampling, you might not pick up on all non-conformities. But over time, with well-planned audits, you can feel confident that you have thoroughly reviewed your system and its performance.

How often to audit

This will depend on you, your business and your business objectives. A rule of thumb is to audit often until the issues are no longer consistent. If people are making the same mistake every week, there are some real concerns.

I advise some of my clients to audit their businesses every week until a level of continuity in the business is clear. I began by auditing every week, then dropped it to every two weeks and now I audit once a month. This fits with the business objectives and the management meetings, where we go through all the managers' audit results – what they did well and what they need to improve on. This helps each manager learn how best to improve their own branch.

However often you decide to audit your business, make sure you stick to the audit schedule. As soon as planned audits start slipping, they lose their power to give the strict procedural guidance that we all need every now and again. Knowing that a regular audit is planned encourages us all to cut corners less often than we would otherwise.

RECAP

In this chapter, you've learned the following.

- The main reasons for carrying out an audit are to:
  - Achieve management priorities
  - Meet regulatory and legislative requirements
  - Audit your suppliers

- Meet customers' individual requirements
- Reduce risks to the organisation.
- The following paperwork is involved:
  - Internal audit schedule
  - Audit checklist
  - Corrective action report
  - Correction action log.
- To carry out an audit:
  - Make sure the auditor is competent
  - Plan the audit
  - Audit effectively.

Task

- Using the documents in the audit process, audit a procedure in your business in as much detail as possible.

- Make sure you use all the forms/check lists to their full potential – it will keep you on track.

FOUR

FEEDBACK

Tell Them What They Did Well
(Or Not)

This is probably the simplest step in the five-part systemisation process, but it rarely happens. This is why.

People don't like confrontation. Even though feedback isn't meant to be confrontational (and I've used the word "confrontation" deliberately), people do see it as such. Telling someone what they did wrong and how they can improve it next time should be a positive experience. Granted, no one likes being told that they haven't done a great job or could do better – I'm having flashbacks to my school reports as I type this – but remember, it's not what you say, it's how you say it.

People don't know what to say. This stems from the confrontation issue. People don't know how to get the point across in such a way that the other person doesn't take offence. We all want to be liked, so we don't enjoy telling someone something that won't please them. But, like anything in life, the more we do it the better we get. The first time I gave negative feedback, it was terrible. I didn't want to look the person in the eye. They got upset, then angry, called me a liar and asked me where the proof was. It was a terrible experience, but I learned from it. First, I thought about how I would have liked to have come across. Then I practised using words and phrases that would help me the next time somebody reacted in a similar way. Thankfully, this didn't happen for quite some time, but when it did, my response was measured and professional. I was able to control the conversation to such a degree that within minutes of getting angry, the employee apologised and said she agreed with the feedback. Her performance dramatically improved as well.

There is little difference between giving audit feedback and giving performance-management feedback. Doing it in the right way is essential to the continuous improvement of the business.

Why give feedback?

There are two main reasons to give feedback.

1. **It helps us improve.** If you think back to the section on what motivates us, it's the desire to be better. Self-actualisation, achievement, attainment, ambition – they're all terms that mean we want to get better at a task, be that at work, in a social situation or in sport. Who wants to run the 1500 metres at the same pace all their life? Who wants to bench-press the same weight forever? No one. We all want to get better at whatever we do. I want to be a better businessman, a better husband and a better dad. Feedback allows us to do exactly that. It shows us what our weak points are, which

gives us the opportunity to improve them. As such, we become better and better.

2. **It improves the company.** If everyone working in a company accepts and understands their feedback and uses it to improve themselves, the company will improve, too. Of course, the company needs to have all its employees heading in the right direction, but the driving force of the company – the board or the owner – also needs to accept feedback so they can change the course of the business and improve.

I was always taught that no one is too big or too bad to be told a few home truths now and again, even if they're not nice to hear. I welcome feedback in all parts of my life. When I was a professional cage fighter and martial artist I was always asking, "That OK, coach?" This wasn't because I needed to be told constantly how good I was – I had a real passion for being the best at whatever I was doing so I needed direction. My wrestling coach, Mick, would tell me if my foot was too wide or if I dropped my hand, and I loved it because it kept me on the right track. Because we had a good relationship, I never took offence from his feedback.

That's the environment or culture you need to build in your organisation. This will happen only if it comes from the top down: the boss needs to accept feedback for others to be able to do so. Building this culture makes for a company that will always strive to improve and use feedback in a positive way.

How to give feedback

There are two types of feedback: positive and negative. Follow these guidelines to give both types of feedback as effectively as possible.

Be direct. Don't beat around the bush. You should give negative and positive feedback in a straightforward way. Being nice and trying not to give bad news wastes time and doesn't do the person waiting for the feedback any favours. Get to the point, be specific and make sure you tell the person what they should do to prevent the problem from happening again.

Be sincere and avoid mixed messages. Sincerity means saying what you mean with care and respect. Mixed messages are "yes, but" messages. Don't use the word "but" when giving feedback. It's either a positive message or a negative one – if you mix them it will confuse the employee.

Focus on the behaviour, not the person. Feedback should never be personal and you should never give that impression, even in your body language. The feedback should always be helpful. Try to explain how the behaviour makes you feel and relate it to the company procedures. For example:

"I've noticed you've been late a few times this week. Is everything OK? I'm worried you might start falling behind in your work, so I need you to start on time." or

"You seem distracted lately, this may have an impact on your work, what can you do to get this back on track?"

Show appreciation when the feedback is good. We all like to be appreciated. If praise is deserved, make sure you give it. It might not be a big deal to you, but it will be to them. They might have been waiting to be appreciated for a while. Remember, employees often seek their manager's approval, especially if that manager is a couple of levels above them. Just think back to how proud you felt at school when the teacher praised your work in front of your classmates. Don't go over the top or be disingenuous, though – make sure the praise is sincere and that you mean it. For example:

"This is really good work, very impressed with your effort, well done."

Show concern when the feedback is bad. If you show concern in your voice, it will communicate a sense of importance to the person receiving the feedback. Showing anger, frustration or disappointment in your tone will turn negative feedback into criticism. Being sarcastic will never get you the response you want – unless that response is anger, frustration or discontent! If your tone is wrong, the meaning of your carefully worded message will be lost. The whole idea of giving negative feedback is to raise awareness of poor performance in a way that leads to better performance. Giving negative feedback in an unhelpful manner defeats the purpose.

Always give feedback face to face. Today, it's easy to give feedback electronically, but I've never been a fan of this. I'm sure you've heard the phrase "people buy from people", and this applies to giving and accepting feedback too. How does it look to the person receiving the feedback if they are of so little importance that you sent it by e-mail? Also, giving feedback isn't just a one-way process. You want your employee to be able to ask questions if they aren't sure about something you've said. Electronic feedback doesn't allow them to ask those real-time questions. Constructive feedback is verbal and informal. That can be done only by talking to an employee face to face – or, if you can't meet in person, over the phone.

Always follow up on the feedback. Never give feedback and then just leave it. Essentially, feedback is the process of saying "This is what you need to do to get better at something". You now need to make sure the person has listened to you, taken on board your feedback and done something about it. Set a time to check that any action points have been carried out. It could be something as simple as a tidy desk or a conversation that the person needs to have with someone. If you don't follow up on the agreed action points, it sends a message that the feedback isn't important and that you're just going through the motions.

Never give sandwich feedback. Sandwich feedback is when you give one bit of negative feedback between two bits of positive feedback. Some people say that it softens the blow of bad news.

My view is that if people need to be given bad feedback in such a way to avoid hurting their feelings, they shouldn't be working for you. A research paper called "The sandwich feedback – not very tasty" by Von Bergen et al looked at this feedback method and found that it wasn't as effective as people first thought:

- It's often used by managers who are afraid to give open and honest feedback.
- It benefits the managers, not the person receiving the feedback.
- It doesn't increase the effectiveness of the feedback.
- It dilutes the main point.

State observations and facts, not interpretations or opinions. Observations are what you see happen; interpretations are your analysis of or opinion on what you see happening. Tell people what you've noticed, not what you think of it. Report the behaviour you notice using concrete facts instead of making judgements. Avoid words and phrases like "I think", "I feel" and "I believe".

When to give feedback

Give feedback as soon as possible. If you take too long to give feedback it loses its strength and impact. After an audit, we always give feedback to managers within a few days so it puts them out of their misery. By "misery", I'm talking about anticipation rather than a sense of doom and gloom. Our managers are competitive so they really look forward to getting feedback. We rank the branches and the managers are keen to see what position theirs are in when the list comes out.

How often to give feedback

How often you should give audit feedback depends on how often you audit the business. You should follow up every audit by giving feedback. There's no point in doing an audit unless you're going to discuss it with people.

There will be situations when, although you wrote everything down in detail when you did audit, you refer back to your notes and think, "What did I mean by that?" or "What was I thinking when I wrote that down?" The sooner you give feedback after you've carried out the audit, the fresher it will be in your mind and the more accurate and relevant it will be.

Feedback paperwork

You don't need to use any complicated forms to record feedback from employees. There's no point having forms for forms' sake – the simpler you can keep it the better. There are plenty available on the internet.

In my business, after the management meeting, which is once a month, the managing director meets with each of the managers and goes through their individual one-to-ones with them. They set targets and talk about what they need to do to hit those targets. They talk about the coming month, but they also talk about the previous month and any audit results. Their feedback is recorded in a one-to-one form, it's very basic and nothing complicated. The managers also get a copy of the non-conformance report so they can see in detail what have been uncovered via the audit and whether they are minor or major. We encourage managers to challenge us about the findings, but this happens rarely. As disappointing as it is for managers to receive a poor audit, they can see that it is fair and they focus on what they can do to put things right.

Whilst this feedback format may differ in your business, find a regular time to speak to your managers or staff and record it as accurately as possible using the forms mentioned. It will help you massively in the long term.

Communication is key

If you take only one thing from this book, please communicate with your staff, whether the feedback is positive or negative. The biggest issue I see in businesses I work with is that people don't talk. We need to communicate to get on in life, to make a coherent ecosystem, to trade, to build relationships, to grow and to be better. If people don't speak to each other, bad feeling boils over and relationships sour. There's an easy fix ... talk to each other!

As mentioned previously, the most difficult thing about giving feedback – initially, at least – is knowing what to say in various circumstances. It's only when we've been in the same situation several times that we become experienced enough to say the right thing every time. My manager at the foundry seemed to be able to charm all the clients and get employees to do whatever he wanted. I asked him how he did that, and all he said was: "When you've done this as long as I have you pick up a thing or two." It wasn't until later that I realised that there's no substitute for getting stuck in, giving it your best shot and learning from your mistakes – and you will make mistakes. Just don't let it put you off trying again, and make sure learn from them.

RECAP

In this chapter, you've learned the following.

- People don't give feedback because:
  - They don't like confrontation
  - They don't know what to say.
- It's important to give feedback because:
  - It helps us to improve
  - It helps the company to improve.
- When giving feedback, it's important to:
  - Be direct
  - Be sincere and avoid mixed messages
  - Show appreciation when feedback is good

- Show concern when feedback is bad
- Always give feedback face to face
- State observations and facts, not interpretations and opinions.

Tasks

- Feed back the results of your audit to one of your staff. If you feel uncomfortable, try it with a family member first. Make sure you go through any objections you think may be brought up. Try role-playing different situations.

- Keep practising. The more you give feedback, the better you'll get at it. Don't shy away from having difficult conversations or giving negative feedback.

- Make sure all feedback is backed up with evidence

FIVE

REVIEW

Work Out What Or Who To Fix!

Based on the results of your internal audit, you'll need to carry out a review. Believe me, you will find something in the audit process, especially as your company gets bigger. I was taught that if you can't find something in the audit, that says more about you as an auditor than it does about the company. It doesn't mean that that your company is outstanding and has done everything completely correctly – it means that you haven't done your audit thoroughly enough to find the non-conformances.

The good news is that you don't need to worry when you do find issues. If you have the mind-set that you're always striving to improve your company, issues that come up in an audit are nuggets of continuous improvement.

The benefit of having a structured review process that's linked to feedback is that there should always be a plan to improve the situation. The purpose of a review is to see where and how you can move forward. Without this part of the process, you'll just keep making the same mistakes, which helps no one. Continual improvement is the key to a successful business, so always strive to move forward.

Sometimes, as business owners, it's hard to review people we have recruited or processes we have implemented. I'll be honest – when we started reviewing my businesses we found several problems that stemmed from things that I had initiated. It was difficult to admit that something I'd put in place had never really worked. As soon as I got over my ego, I recognised that I shouldn't view this as a failure but as a step towards finding a better process. After that, I felt much better about reviewing people I had employed or procedures I had written.

In my company, I've reached the stage, a few years ago, where my team reviews the people and processes. This makes everything much easier and more efficient for me. This will happen to you too: the larger your organisation becomes, the less time you'll be spending "pulling out the weeds". Your employees will drive continual improvement forward for you, and the review process is integral to this.

Person or process?

There are two main types of issues in a business: people issues and process issues. As a reviewer, it's your job to use the facts and evidence to determine who or what is at fault and identify the right course of action to prevent an issue happening again.

The main objective of systemisation is the continuous improvement of the business. You need to be aware that, depending on your findings, people may lose their jobs, departments may be closed and projects may be shelved. You need to be brutally honest. While the immediate action that comes out of the review may seem negative, the overarching strategic goal is to improve the company and keep it moving forward. That, in itself, is positive.

You need to be mindful of the reason for, or the root cause of, the issue. On the face of it, it could look as if an employee is not achieving what's expected of them or is involved in the same issue again and again. Some people will assume that this is a people issue and that the employee needs to be more motivated or learn new skills. Some may even say that performance management is needed or that their employment should be terminated. This is a knee-jerk reaction. We need to use what the academics call critical analysis to understand the whole issue and find its root cause.

Root-cause analysis

I've heard this being called investigation analysis and failure analysis, among other things, but they are essentially the same. To analyse the root cause, you need to ask three questions:

1. What's the issue or problem?
2. Why did it happen (what caused it)?
3. What do we need to do to stop it happening again?

Without going too far into root-cause analysis and problem-solving, which is a book in itself, I will share a simple but effective technique that I use. I've never come across a problem that this technique has not been able to help me solve.

The five whys

This technique was first used by Sakichi Toyoda, one of the founders of the Japanese industrial revolution. Although he developed the technique back in the 1930s, it became popular in the 1970s and Toyota still uses it today. We use it a lot in our businesses, with great effect.

It's basically asking when something goes wrong, "Why did this happen in this situation?" When you get the answer, you ask, "But why did that happen?" – then again and again and again, really getting to the root cause of the issue. By the fifth time you have, in most cases, gone back to the absolute beginning of the issue and can deal with the cause rather than one of the effects. It's a very powerful tool to use in your business.

Some people don't use this as they don't want to uncover the underlying issue of problems. The five whys get to the bottom of the problem. Without knowing what caused the issue, it is very hard to rectify.

The advantage of the five whys is that it gives a structure for problem-solving while allowing us to focus on the immediate issue at hand. If you've attended senior management or board meetings, you'll know that people start giving opinions that aren't based on facts and quickly meander off the topic. This leads to an unproductive and frustrating meeting. The five whys keep everyone on-topic and force us to think about a solution to the problem. In my experience, this halves the time needed to resolve the issue. That's a huge amount of time saved, and time is a precious commodity in business.

In my experience, people quickly get used to the five whys. They start looking for solutions to issues before meetings so they have the answers ready. I call this process "level up thinking". We want our staff to start thinking like a level above their role. The portfolio managers start thinking like the branch managers and the branch managers start thinking like the area manager, and so on. It's a change of mind-set and is a huge help when following the company procedures.

If you're into lean six sigma or lean manufacturing which is all about making your business as efficient as possible , you might have heard the following story. There are several, slightly different versions out there.

At the Jefferson Memorial in Washington DC, there was a problem. Sparrows were defecating all over the memorial. This was making it unpleasant for visitors, many of whom had travelled from all over the world.

To make things worse, the excessive water and detergent used to clean up the mess was damaging the monument – so much so that in May 1990 a fifty-pound block of marble fell from the monument. Luckily, no one was hurt.

Those responsible for the monument wanted to know why they were facing these issues. The report, which allegedly cost nearly two million dollars, was startling.

The birds were attracted to the Jefferson Memorial because of the abundance of spiders – the staple diet for birds. The spiders were attracted to the memorial because of the midges (insects) that were nesting there. The midges were nesting there because of the light. Midges, it turns out, like to procreate in places were the light is just right – and because the lights were turned on at the Jefferson Memorial one hour before dark, it created the kind of mood lighting that midges went crazy for.

How did they resolve the situation? After reviewing the curious chain of events that led to the problem, and by asking the five whys, the decision was made to wait until dark before switching on the lights at the Jefferson Memorial. The one-hour delay stopped the midges from congregating around the memorial for some romance. This, in turn, stopped the spiders, which stopped the birds... which sorted out the problem with the droppings.

There is a little more to the story, which adds weight to the concept of the five whys. The park, although aware of the suggestion of delaying switching on the lights for an hour, tried other methods first because they thought that delaying lighting up the monument would lead to complaints from photographers. Other, more expensive solutions were discussed, such as hiring more staff to clean the memorial, experimenting with less abrasive cleaning materials or even closing the monument to the public. It took five years and millions of dollars before they accepted the original suggestion.

So a simple and cost-saving solution, in the end, was found just by asking a probing question.

Practise the five whys with your team as often as possible so they get used to it. This will help you find the best solutions as easily as possible during your review process. This is without doubt the most effective technique I use for reviewing audits. Everybody knows what they're aiming for and it forces them to dive into the issues. It creates a culture in the business.

When to review

The best time to carry out a review of the audit is straight afterwards, when everything is fresh in your mind. No matter how comprehensive your notes, you won't have written everything down and something, even if it's only small, will get missed if you delay the review. If you wait months or even just weeks to look back at your notes, you'll find you won't remember everything.

After every audit, discuss the issues and find any solutions necessary.

Who to involve

Like many large companies, Toyota has a "go and see" policy. This is where the senior decision-makers go out onto the shop floor and see processes in action. You can't come up with a solution to a major process issue by sitting in a board room – you need to see how the process really works.

I speak to everybody involved in the process, from the cleaner right through to the finance director if necessary. Everybody's opinions are equally valuable and no suggestion is a silly one. I thank people for their suggestions and never make fun or jest. If I don't agree, I always explain why. It's good to encourage employees to come forward with possible solutions to issues, not to embarrass them into silence.

Review paperwork

You need just one document to control all your review changes – a review action log. It's important to record these changes so you can spot any trends. For example, you might be constantly writing unrealistic procedures or people issues might be becoming all too common. It's surprising what information you can glean from the data you record. An example log is shown below.

No	Action Item	Responsible individual	Due Date	Completion Date
Review Action Log			Form: 32	
			Revision: 02	
1				
2				
3				
4				
5				
6				
7				
8				
9				
10				
11				
12				
13				

Action item. Include as much detail as you can about the action identified in the review so that nothing is missed.

Responsible individual. Who is responsible for carrying out the task? Is it more than one person? Only include the name of the person with overall responsibility here. It may be a five- or even a ten-person job, but from an organisational point of view you want one person taking the lead.

Due date and completion date. Nothing surprising here. Always use dates to hold people accountable and ensure targets are met. Without target dates, people won't prioritise things and they won't get done.

During every review or management meeting, distribute the agreed action log. This makes sure everyone is aware that they must complete their actions in the allotted time.

This review process may seem like a lot of work, and some of you might not think it's worth the effort. But reviewing your business on a regular basis, including audit reviews, is essential to continuous improvement and staying ahead of the competition. You'll find issues in your business that you didn't know existed. You'll come up with ways to make good processes even better. You'll improve employee satisfaction by listening to them. And your customers will feel the benefit of all this.

RECAP

In this chapter, you've learned the following.

- When things go wrong it is only ever a person or process issue.
- Use root-cause analysis to help you review. Use the five whys as a tool.
- The best time to review is straight after the audit.
- Involve everyone in your review.
- Use a review action template.

Task

- Look at a procedure that didn't go to plan. Use the five whys to drill down to the basic questions of what happened and why. Practise this with as many issues as you can to become as effective as possible.

- When using the five whys you need to be firm in your approach. Your staff, at first, will try and ignore the five whys and go off on tangents. It is your job to keep everyone focused and on track.

SIX

MAKE IT WORK

Develop A
Leadership-centric Business

I've mentioned several times that other people run my business and other ventures. This is by design. Yes, I had to put the work in at the start to build the business up and recruit a leader, but I had to either find someone else to lead the company or carry on doing it myself. You need a captain to sail a ship, a pilot to fly a plane and a leader to drive a business forward. You can't build multiple businesses and run them all yourself.

You can have the best systems in the world, an auditing process to be proud of and a feedback loop that would make Disney proud – but without identifying a leader to take control of the organisation, you're still a slave to the business.

One of the main purposes of having a systemised company is that you don't have to work if you don't want to. This only works if you have someone else to lead the company and take it forward. Having a systemised business is all about choices, and having a leader gives you those choices. They handle all the issues with staff, customers, finances and so on. it's the real secret to scaling up your business.

So why do people find it so hard to appoint a leader? It's down to a combination of things. Business owners can be precious about their businesses, and I understand that. I used to be like that. They look for exact replicas of themselves, and that's a huge mistake.

It's never going to happen. There is only one you, and thank goodness for that. Imagine two John Pauls or two of you. I couldn't think of anything worse. People say when two people are too alike, they argue and quibble. This would be no different. Instead of letting go, you would micro-manage and cause friction and frustration.

My managing director is different from me. That's a good thing. She brings perspective to things that I would normally go charging into. She asks questions and challenges me about situations where I thought that my way was the right way. This has changed my take on things and certainly improved me as a business man. You don't want a carbon copy of yourself–, you want, and need, someone who will disagree with you and challenge you. This improves the decision-making process.

Many business owners are not great at critical analysis – that is, looking at both sides of the story. They're used to doing things their own way and being the ones to make the decisions in their business. A leader who is not identical to you will improve the critical-analysis skills in your leadership toolkit and make you a better businessperson and a better leader. They will improve your empathy, self-regulation and self-awareness; in other words, they'll improve your emotional intelligence.

What do I look for in a potential leader?

Look for the following attributes.

Someone who lives and breathes the organisation. If someone is perfectly aligned to your company vision and values, they already show a huge amount of potential.

Finding someone who shares these things is important. If you have a great training and development process, you can teach skills and make people capable, but you can't force them to believe what you believe. Employees must choose to buy in to it themselves. Vision is vital to the success of a company. Having a leader whose values align with that vision helps to get buy-in from employees and makes the leader's job much easier. If you can identify someone who shares your vision then you don't have to worry about them making a decision you would strongly disagree with or that would put your company or reputation in jeopardy.

I share the same vision and values as my managing director, so I'm completely at ease with her making decisions in the business. I know she will always have the best interests of the company, the staff and me at heart. Because I never have to worry whether she has done something that isn't aligned with the company's vision, that frees me up to work on new ventures and look for new opportunities. In turn, that generates more income for the business. It's a virtuous cycle.

A good example of someone not sharing the same vision and values is Jordan Belfort, known as the "Wolf of Wall Street". Was he good at his job? The answer is yes, as he made a lot of people a lot of money. Would you invest with him? Personally, I would never consider investing with him, as his values are different from mine.

Potential, not performance. Not everyone performs at their best from day one, and to be the best version of yourself takes years to achieve. If you're looking for a leader who's already the best, this may be a long process and you might never identify that person.

Potential is a totally different thing. You want someone who has room to grow and, more importantly, who is willing to grow. Again, this is not hard to identify. Look for people who are hungry to learn and who are determined to make themselves better at their job. This is half the battle and is the foundation of a true leader. These people accept that they are not the finished article, they accept that they have a way to go, and they always strive to be a better version of themselves.

Emotional intelligence. As I mentioned in the introduction to this chapter, emotional intelligence is essential to being a better and more effective leader. It can improve your own leadership development and help you identify real leadership potential in others.

Daniel Goleman brought emotional intelligence into the mainstream in 1995, but it was first mentioned in 1964 in a paper by Michael Beldoch. In a nutshell, emotional intelligence is the capacity to recognise your own and other people's emotions. The best leaders score highly in the following attributes: social skills, empathy, self-regulation, self-awareness and motivation. Look for those attributes in your potential leader.

It stands to reason that if you can connect with others on a more emotional level, you will build better relationships and get better results. Those who don't connect or don't realise when their colleagues or employees are struggling are seen as non-empathetic. Do you ever hear employees say "He just doesn't get me", "He doesn't know what I'm going through" or "She just doesn't understand"? In my experience, when a member of staff says this on more than one occasion it's not them who is the issue – it's my lack of emotional understanding.

Look for potential leaders with high levels of emotional intelligence.

Communication skills. Great leaders are great communicators. If you look at the vast majority of leaders in business and in sport, the best performers are good communicators. Martin Johnson, the England rugby captain whose team won the 2003 Rugby World Cup, is a great example. As captain, he led from the front and, importantly, he got buy-in from the other players. Communication played a big part in this. If you don't communicate, people can't buy in to your vision and values. People buy people, and those who don't communicate take longer to be bought. This is a problem when time is an issue.

Communication isn't all one-way. Great leaders ask for feedback and listen as much as, if not more than, they talk. The message loses its impact if it goes on longer than it needs to. It's the same with leaders. A few carefully chosen words have the greatest impact.

Remember, you're not expecting to find a communicator like Winston Churchill, an orator who stirred the soul, to lead your business. But, as always, you can spot someone with great potential who is keen to improve themselves.

Ability to stay calm. All good leaders stay calm in difficult situations. They always seem to know what to do, they always have the right answers, they never sweat or get flustered ... or do they? Of course they do – they just don't show it. Everyone gets nervous before a big event or a big decision. It's human nature; it's in our biology. Anyone who says otherwise is saying so for bravado.

The only difference with great leaders is that they understand that appearing to be calm instils confidence in their followers. No one wants to follow a leader who panics and doesn't seem to know what to do.

I've been in situations in business, in sport and in life when I didn't have all the answers and didn't know what to do. But one thing I've never done is show panic. I calmly address the situation. If I need a bit more time to review it, I take that time. I make sure that I make the right decision and that I don't get rushed into things when I don't have all the facts.

The attribute of keeping calm while under fire is an important one. If any of your employees show this trait, they could be on their way to becoming a great business leader. Be mindful, though, that there is a difference between calmness and not caring. I've seen some people react to a situation with apparent calmness when in fact they just didn't care. There's a huge difference.

Challenge your leader

You want the best for your business, don't you? You want to find a leader who's the best fit. In any walk of life, you want to do your best (at least, you should), and the only way to keep improving is to let yourself be challenged.

Think about it. In sport, we get better by playing better teams or training with better people. At school, we get better as the lesson content gets harder and the exams become more challenging. This helps us grow and become better versions of ourselves.

If you perform the same role over and over again, you should become more effective and efficient at that particular role. But you won't feel challenged and you'll eventually become bored or complacent. As I've mentioned previously, it's the steady progression in ability and responsibility that truly motivates people. So, challenging them is how you get the best from them.

Push your potential leader to become better. You need to strike a balance, of course – don't overwhelm them by giving them too many responsibilities or putting them under pressure when they haven't had the training and development they need to achieve the organisational goals.

Empowering someone and abdicating responsibility are two different things. Empower someone to lead, and it will enhance the confidence of a valuable member of staff. Simply abdicate responsibility (palm off your duties) and it will demotivate and demoralise the employee; it may even force them to leave the company. This is where you need to use your emotional intelligence to empathise with others and be aware of your own strengths and weaknesses. Abdicating your own responsibilities will be seen in a negative light, so make sure you are clear when you delegate responsibilities to your potential leader.

Make sure you challenge your potential leader not only by increasing their workload but also by delegating more difficult work. Dumping twice as much filing on someone will be challenging in terms of getting it all done in time, but it won't get the grey matter moving or motivate them.

When you challenge your employees, especially prospective leaders, make the tasks more difficult and put slightly more pressure on them to see how they react. As the saying goes, you have to be cruel to be kind. It's no good telling your son he's excellent at football so he can take it easy and then putting him into a Saturday game where he gets shown up. He'll never thank you for that. The same applies in business, except in this case people can lose their jobs if they make mistakes. That means it's even more important to make sure you have the right person in the right role and that they are performing well.

Develop a training programme

As mentioned earlier, any training and development programme needs to be thoroughly planned and documented, no matter who you're training. I have an ILP and I follow it religiously. I also make sure I'm accountable to my managing director and to my better half, Gemma. They check that I'm progressing towards my goals – completing the courses I start and upskilling myself in the ways I have identified.

Make sure your prospective leader has an ILP. No matter how small you think the milestones are, make sure you document them in detail. I'm a huge fan of ILPs, as they show us where we are on our progression journey and whether we need any extra support. They also allow us to celebrate our mini successes, which I think we should do.

Your programme should be challenging. It should push your prospective leader to achieve their own goals and the company goals. Never adjust your goals to make them easier for your leader to attain. The leader needs to up their game to achieve your organisational goals and meet company standards.

When developing a training plan, communication is the key. You need to have open communication with your prospective leader. Sit down with them and go over all the training you expect them to achieve and how that fits into the overall business strategy. I believe you get better buy-in from all employees when they can see where they fit in to the larger picture.

This isn't a Mr Miyagi situation, where you don't tell the person why they're doing something and hope that it will all fit together in the end. Communicate with your prospective leader – be open and honest about their training and development and support them as they grow and progress.

Learn to let go – and be patient

Letting go is hard to do, as it goes against our primal instinct to be in control. The hardest thing I had to do in business was let go and trust my staff, but the belief that no one could do the job better than I could was arrogant and, in some respects, wrong. If you ask my staff, they will certainly tell you I was wrong. I felt that my employees wouldn't care as much as I did or share the passion that

I had. In some instances, that was true, but the question I had to ask myself was whether the stronger passion I had would guarantee more business. Of course, it wouldn't, so why continue to struggle to do everything myself?

One thing it did do was stress me out. I didn't have a business, I had a job – and a stressful and badly paid one at that.

If I had recruited correctly in the first place, my employees would have shared my vision, values and beliefs and would ultimately have done as good a job as me, if not better. I have now created a culture that we can all be proud of.

Letting go is a matter of changing your mind-set rather than a physical process, although the sweaty palms and sleepless nights might tell a different story! It's important to understand that your staff will make mistakes. They will mess up and you'll want to take back control from them. Don't. If you pick nothing else up from this chapter, please have the confidence to trust your employees and your chosen leader and their ability to do their job. If you've recruited your prospective leader well, you've trained and developed them and they share the company's vision, values and beliefs, you just need to give them time to grow and turn into the leader you want to create.

No one plays football on a Sunday morning and signs up for Sunderland the following week (no one wants to play for Sunderland, but that's a different matter). People need time to learn, to grow and to make mistakes. Of course, you don't *want* your employees to make mistakes, and you want to prepare them as best you can to run or take over your organisation. But when you delegate responsibility, people will screw up sometimes. You just have to accept that.

For me, the pros of having a leader in the business far outweigh the cons of going through the growing pains – not that I had many. It's satisfying to see your employee get better and better each day and become the leader you are hoping for. Did my managing director make mistakes at first? Of course she did. Did she learn from them? Yes, definitely. At times, I wanted to take back some aspects of the role, believing that I could do a better job, but that would have been demotivating and would have sent out the wrong message.

I sat back and let Adele grow into the role to such an extent that she is now a better manager than I could ever hope to be. I was there to help and support her in any way I could but I had to let go, let her get on with it and be patient.

Let everyone know you have a leader

If you systemise your business effectively and train and develop your leader, they will eventually be in a position to run the business. Now it's time to let people know. Most importantly, this shows your leader that you trust them and that you're empowering them to run and lead your organisation. You may already say behind closed doors that your leader is running the business, but nothing will say it more clearly than when you, as the business owner, give all the credit to your leader in public. This will give you massive buy-in from your leader and they'll appreciate you for giving credit where it's due.

John Maxwell, a leadership and management expert, wrote a book called "*5 Levels of Leadership*". In essence, the five levels represent different stages in a person's leadership and management career. Many people never get past level 2, as most leaders are only leaders by title: they are not true leaders. Level 4 is all about people development, which is when what makes you a better leader is what you do for other people. In the context of appointing someone to lead your company, you are making that person a leader in your organisation. Because you are doing something for them, stating this publicly automatically moves you up the leadership staircase.

Letting other people know you have a leader also frees you from doing certain leadership activities that you no longer want to do, which saves you time. For example, if someone wants to talk about a new opportunity or wants to sell me something, I point them in the direction of my managing director. She filters the opportunities and presents me with any that need my input. Much of this type of stuff doesn't interest me, especially things like IT and phones, but these things are essential to operations. As Adele is more hands-on as a leader, she is better at this task. She comes up with a list of the best three and then we speak about it. You can let everyone know that your leader is the right person to deal with for certain things. Once they've implemented something and it's working well, you can give them the credit.

What happens if I train someone and they leave?

That's a good question, but what happens if you don't train them and they stay? You only want the best people working for you – otherwise, you're not running a workplace, you're running a crèche, babysitting everyone and spending your time sticking up for them.

If you want demotivated staff, poor customer service, constant firefighting, no time to yourself and no profit, don't train and develop your staff in leadership. I doubt that will appeal to you.

Developing that leader in your business will not happen overnight. It's a long and difficult process and yes, there is a risk that they'll leave after you've trained them up. But if you've created a culture of being better, you'll have someone else who's ready to take their place. You'll have a conveyer belt of potential leaders in the business. Some will leave, as there won't be enough progression routes for everyone, but it's far better to train and develop people who leave than have a team of demotivated, uninspiring plodders who only want to work from 9am to 5pm. There's nothing wrong with plodders – every business needs them – but you don't want a payroll that's full of them.

Leadership is turning vision into reality using influence to create followers.

CONCLUSION

The five-part systemisation framework needs to be a way of life for you and your business if you want to reap the rewards of what a truly systemised business can do for you. It's a bit like a rugby or football tackle: if you don't give it your best effort, you could get hurt (metaphorically speaking, of course).

In business, you go hard or go home. This is especially true when you employ people and you're responsible for providing for other families as well as your own. This is a great privilege, and you should never take it for granted. You can only achieve real success when you take your business seriously and make it sustainable.

Notice that I haven't said that you need to make your company a big business. That might not be your passion and it might not be in line with your values. But all businesses should be safe and sustainable environments where people can do their best and have a career for life if they choose. Systems will give you that sustainability. All you need to do is follow the five-part systemisation framework to improve the running of your business.

I speak from personal experience when I say that bad things happen for no good reason. To ensure your family, legacy and staff are safe and well looked after, systems are a must. I can't imagine any business owner wanting to leave a troubled organisation to their next of kin. You want to leave an income-generating, valuable asset to your family – something they will thank you for and that will make them proud of you.

You probably want to exit your business long before that stage so you can enjoy other things in your life. No one wants to be the richest man in the graveyard. We all want to spend more time doing things we love. The majority of business owners and entrepreneurs I know want to exit while they're still young enough to enjoy the results of all their years of hard work.

You simply can't do this without systems. I don't know a successful business that doesn't have systems of some description.

I hope this book has shown you how to systemise your business and explained the benefits it can bring. For more tips and resources, please visit my website at www.the5partsystem.com.

THE AUTHOR

John Paul is an entrepreneur, leader and owner of the Castledene Group, an award-winning sales and letting agency based in north-east England. Widely regarded as one of the leading experts in the property industry, John won the *Sunday Times* Outstanding Contribution to Lettings Award in 2015 and speaks at networking events all over the UK. John has grown Castledene Sales and Lettings into six branches employing fifty staff. Thanks to the five-part system, he no longer has anything to do with the day-to-day operations of the company. Through The Property and Leadership Academy he aims to improve management and leadership within the industry and consults with many companies around the UK. In doing so he helps people to systemise their businesses and make themselves non-integral to the running of the business.

John is also on the Board of the Association of Residential Letting Agents (ARLA), representing the North of England. He has also just started his Masters in Leadership.

John has three amazing children – Stephanie, Jack and Bella – and a long-suffering but supportive partner, Gemma. They live in Redmarshall in Stockton on Tees.

If you would like to know more or contact John, please e-mail him at johnpaul@thecastledenegroup.com or visit the website www.the5partsystem.com.